THE POLITICS OF PUBLIC HIGHER EDUCATION

STRATEGIC DECISIONS FORGED FROM CONSTITUENCY COMPETITION, COOPERATION, AND COMPROMISE

TOM ANDERES

PAGE PUBLISHING, INC.
New York, NY

First originally published by Page Publishing, Inc. 2019

ISBN 978-1-64544-704-7 (Paperback)
ISBN 978-1-64544-705-4 (Digital)

Printed in the United States of America

To my three sons, Mike, Jeff, and Eric, and their
wonderful wives and exceptional children.

CONTENTS

OVERVIEW

THIS BOOK WILL focus on the many constituencies who actively, and often aggressively, engage in the politics of planning, delivery, and consumption of public higher education. The goal of the book is to give the reader a clear picture of the interaction, both directly and indirectly, of various constituencies as they seek to advance their positions on the key issues that confront public higher education. (An emphasis is placed on *public* higher education because of the role of state government in funding and providing various levels of oversight for the delivery programs and services.) The amount and intensity of the interaction will help in assessing why various decisions are implemented. The ultimate value will be to provide leaders with the concepts and examples they can apply in their everyday decision-making. They can "test" their positions, processes, and alternative scenarios against situations that others have experienced.

The term *politics* often has a different meaning based on the perspective of a given constituency, such as the governor, legislator, student, faculty member, board leadership, etc. It is critical to define and isolate the types and consequences of politics based on the statements, positions, and actions taken by various constituencies who inform leaders as they consider their institutions future.

The reader will benefit from the use of the Strategic Decision-Making Model (SDMM), defined and discussed in *Planning, Policy and Politics: Tools to Help Leaders Make Strategic Choices* (Anderes 2016), to help understand and manage the consequences of actions affecting leader's strategic decisions. This book puts a greater emphasis on the specifics of constituency relationships, how the relationships evolve, and the interaction of internal and external politics that are apparent at every level of government. Politics permeates institutions of higher education, systems of higher education, the governor's oversight role, the legislature, and other external agencies that have some involvement in higher education decision-making. The politics of internal (within higher education) decision-making versus external oversight (governor and legislature) are different in form and substance. They also have many common characteristics and often intersect and clash over substantive differences in their relative priorities and values.

Competition

The list of higher education constituents (those having direct and indirect involvement with higher education) is very broad, ranging from students, faculty, and higher education leaders to governors, legislators, and other state officials. Also included would be the public, federal government, accrediting agencies, and other groups having varying levels of interest in higher education process, goals, and outcomes. The primary constituencies will be defined and compared against others to assess the relative positions on specific scenarios. The comparisons in priorities and positions often reflect intense competition. The competition arises when multiple interest groups clash due to disagreements over what is most important within an organization, institution, higher education system, or state. Differences are magnified based on what each sees as the appropriate remedy given their own unique perspectives. This book will help in understanding the nature of the competition and why compromise is frequently the only viable, albeit messy, means for change. It will show how alternative solutions can be developed that incorporate the many ramifications of the key goals and issues of higher education leaders and their constituencies.

Politics

The term *politics* will be defined from a number of sources to clarify the extent to which constituent input helps shape decisions. The decisions, as will be seen through different scenarios, are rarely made that reflect a solution supported by one constituent group. Decisions of importance to students, faculty, leaders, and others, internal and external to an institution, often represent a series of compromises necessary to gain sufficient support for agreement and implementation. While compromise alters each constituency's optimal solutions, they do provide a pathway to recognize existing inequities or limit areas of difference. Compromise may even spawn temporary alliances between opposing constituencies that creates support for a given issue. Success is often unpredictable given a host of conditions that constituencies will find acceptable at one time but not at another.

Constituencies

The book will examine the interplay of constituencies that are internal to a university or community college and those falling outside of a public system or institution. The differences between internal and external constituents are significant, and as might be expected, so are their relative views on the most important priorities. The book will dedicate a chapter to each constituency that will focus on their interaction and influence on one another. How they work with or in opposition to one another will be tested through the use of scenarios that offer different challenges and test their capacity to work cooperatively or competitively. The politics of constituent competition and the degree to which there is compromise will be emphasized in each chapter.

Complexity of Decision-Making

The collective influence of politics on constituencies is driven by many key issues. The issues will be raised with the understanding that outcomes will vary year to year based on the relative weight of the political variables in play. If the legislature reduces higher education funding in one year over the objections of the governor, then in the next year, there may be an increase in funding for higher education based on any combination of factors. Increased funding may be recommended as an outcome of added state revenues or the impact of public dissent due to steep tuition increases (driven by prior years lower state funding), or university threats to reduce access, or concerns for accreditation downgrades in various programs. This simple example highlights the interplay of variables driven by different constituencies of higher education. Politics at the institutional system (multi-institutional oversight) and state levels shape the priorities and resource decisions made by higher education leaders.

The complexity for decision makers increases based on the number of constituencies seeking recognition, the number of issues being resolved through multiparty compromises and the number of years to address constituent expectations. As an example, given limitations on the state being able to fund multiple constituencies at desired levels, there could be financial or other considerations promised over many years. The multiyear considerations or "agreements" to satisfy constituent demands would be based on priorities generated through internal and external negotiations, ideally with gubernatorial and legislative leaders' continuing support. The original agreements may be modified or even suspended depending on changing political conditions (e.g., altered state priorities, reduced state funding, demands for increased efficiencies, and other concessions). The primary point to be made is that complexity can move boundaries beyond annual or biennial sessions to attain a successful compromise.

Many factors drive complexity for all constituencies, including gubernatorial and legislative turnover, philosophical shifts in governmental support, financial limitations, constituent aggressiveness, realignment of higher education priorities, unforeseen disruptions, and many more intervening events. This book will reflect on the complexity of decision-making and how leaders can be better informed in rapidly evolving local, state, and global environments. The greater the capacity of leaders to understand the environments within which their programs thrive or fail and the multitude of expectations driven by constituencies, the greater their ability to offer meaningful decisions reflecting the clearest path into the future.

A final chapter will provide a scenario based on a complex set of problems and conditions that will push constituencies to act, interact, and react in seeking solutions that best meet their individual programs. It will force each constituency to compete, cooperate and compromise where possible and, if not possible, seek the best outcome regardless of implications for others. It will draw from tools of the SDMM to navigate through the internal and external politics and arrive at an alternative solution for leadership consideration.

A Method to Assess the Influence of Politics on Decision-Making

A framework will be provided at the outset of the book as a guide to better understand the often-imperfect balance of competing demands among constituencies that lead to equally imperfect forms of compromise. The balance may tip in different directions year to year and generate seemingly incongruous compromises when viewed over time. The value of applying an objective framework that helps guide leaders toward the most thoughtful decisions becomes increasingly more important.

One of the tools presented in the book *Planning, Policy and Politics in Higher Education: Tools to Help Leaders Make Strategic Choices* (Anderes 2016) is the SDMM. It was created to capture relevant information originating from and being debated by internal and external constituencies. The model supports extensive communication avenues for the exploration of key goals and issues, historical realities, potential futures (through the use of future scans), constituent expectations, and financial analyses, all examined through comprehensive strategic planning processes. The major goal is to aggregate all the information in a manner that provides leaders with alternative solutions or strategies representing precursors to final decision-making. The final decisions would represent a hybrid of various positions debated throughout the process and ultimately support leadership priorities as they are approved by governing boards. In many instances, those decisions would be transformed into institutional and system priorities for submission as planning, policy, or funding requests to governors and legislatures. It is critical that the planning process be initiated by leadership, be defined through constituent debate, and generate quality inputs supporting strategic outcomes. Constituent expectations must be actively addressed through the various layers of the SDMM.

The primary takeaway is that the SDMM wraps the influences of politics into the fabric of the process. Final decisions should reflect the implications of the political past and future for constituencies to ensure transparency and a willingness to clarify why the choices were made. The lack of communications regarding key decisions will only engender hard feelings and future resistance by those constituents that feel their voice was not heard.

The diminished support for public higher education over the last decade has placed greater and greater pressure on leaders to establish processes for input and debate prior to decision-making. They have been asked to be more accountable while dealing with fewer and fewer state dollars. The irony of providing more justification for reduced funds is obvious, yet every dollar received from the state is one less that has to be charged to the student. Even fewer state funds are better than nothing!

Structure of the Book

Various definitions of politics and constituency lay the foundation from which one can understand the complex relationship between constituencies on issues of importance in higher education. It is necessary to understand what a constituency is and its role in engaging in politics. The interrelationship of constituencies with varying agendas and priorities in higher education will be one focus of the book. The reality of competition, cooperation, and compromise among interest groups vying for recognition is the essence of politics. Politics represents the exchange of views, resources, promises for future value, denials of past intransigencies, approval of immediate demands, and a host of other evenly and unevenly balanced expectations. The expectations are magnified within a highly competitive environment characterized by constituents having strongly held beliefs on the relative (and often conflicting) values in addressing the most important goals of public higher education.

The following provides some background on each chapter in the book. It is a brief glimpse of the content and connections of how decisions are made based on constituent interactions. Each chapter brings a different layer of information to the complexities of competition, cooperation, and compromise. The layers are based on different scenarios that raise multiple problems and conditions that higher education leaders must create thoughtful and strategic responses. The responses should address the implications of the conditions in a manner that recognizes internal and external constituency expectations while maintaining a clear connection to the primary goals and strategic directions of the higher education enterprise.

The SDMM creates a framework through which those complexities can be sorted, assessed, and understood in a way that brings meaning and value to planners and decision makers. Chapters 1 and 4-11 will use the planning-and-assessment framework. (P-and-A framework), one component of the SDMM, as the tool to review and assess each scenario. The full model, through each of its six components, will be applied in chapter 12 on the final and most complex scenario to give the reader a comprehensive understanding for the inter connection of the components in supporting leadership decision-making.

The full model is not used in each chapter given the sheer amount of information and analyses required for each of the scenarios. *It will be reemphasized throughout the book that all six components must be applied by an institution or system to create the most-informed decisions possible.* The use of the P and A framework is simply the one component that will allow for an assessment of each scenario in addressing the conditions laid out in the scenario. It should be remembered that the information reviewed and assessed by the P and A framework is derived from other model components and relies on the full interaction of those components to develop meaningful analyses and alternatives.

Brief summaries of the chapters are the following:

Chapter 1—Assessing What Influences Constituencies: Applying the Strategic Decision-Making Model

Chapter 1 lays out the premise of the book with attention paid to the symbiotic relationship of politics and constituency demand. The relationships will be highlighted by a scenario that is filtered through the P and A framework, one of the key components of the SDMM. The assessment produces three alternatives that leaders could choose from based on their reading of how successful each would be based on their interpretation of the environment. An important point in this chapter and in others is that different leaders will make different decisions based on what their perspective is on what must be achieved, when it must be achieved, and who will benefit most and least. How one leader weighs the value of a set of conditions versus another leader will depend on their goals and expectations going into a strategic planning process and how those expectations may have changed by the end of the process. It is inevitable that a different alternative will suit one leader better than another, considering variations in their respective decision-making environments.

It is not uncommon for people to view politics as a mixture of short-term vision, and high-cost services that don't benefit all citizens equally. There is a distrust based on power being held by a few who do not represent the majority. Various constituencies or interest groups are in an ongoing battle to gain their share (or an increase) of the resources controlled by politicians and bureaucrats. They seek to influence those with the power to support their cause.

We will discuss how planners and leaders can make choices that strategically consider organizational goals, political realities, and constituent expectations. The SDMM and specifically the planning and assessment framework will guide the discussion that seeks to balance politics and constituent expectations.

(This chapter precedes chapters two and three that define politics and constituency, respectively, because it is intended to outline the SDMM as the primary means through which politics, constituency, competition, cooperation, and compromise will be compared, contrasted, and assessed.)

Chapter 2—What Is Politics and How Does It Influence Decision-Making?

Politics will be defined and discussed in a way that recognizes the interaction of constituencies interested in the same issues but not necessarily always agreeing on goals, timing, outcomes, costs, etc. Detail will be offered on the context of politics generally and specifically as it influences leaders in the strategic choices they consider and eventually support.

A primary goal of the chapter is to highlight that politics is not simply an artifact of the local, state, and national elections. It is more importantly the ongoing interaction of all constituencies in influencing how and when decisions are made. Higher education constituencies such as students, faculty, higher education leaders, and boards of higher education are continuously interacting with not only legislative and executive staff but also the public, and other internal and external interest groups, when considering what actions to take on given issues.

The distinction between big-P politics, as we ascribe to legislators and the governor, and little-p politics, represented by the myriad of higher education constituencies seeking to influence those who will affect their programs, is key. The essence of competition, cooperation, and compromise is inextricably connected to constituency interaction. It is the intensity of interaction among the big-P and little-p actors that will define the timing, cost, and outcomes. The actions of internal constituencies will be connected with the little-p politics, while external constituencies, or big-P politics, will be aligned with the governor, the legislature, and other external groups. The term *big-P politics* will be used interchangeably with external politics, while *little-p politics* will be linked to internal politics.

Chapter 3—What Are the Constituencies That Influence Higher Education?

Who are the constituencies connected to higher education, and what is their importance in leadership decision-making? While the focus of the book is on politics, it will be clear that each constituent represents a subset of many units vying for recognition and resources. Why are they important in the planning, financing, assessing, and influencing the ultimate outcomes of public higher education?

There are many constituencies interested in higher education. There are those who are invested in and want to expand higher education programming. There are others who are more interested in other state priorities and limiting the amount of funding going to higher education. The concepts of big-P politics as represented by the governor and legislature primarily and little-p politics representing faculty, staff, students, higher education leaders, and other internal constituencies defined in this chapter will be used liberally throughout the book. It is the dynamic of internal (inside higher education) interactions of constituencies in building higher education programs and then the interactions of the internal constituencies with the governor and legislature in gaining support for those programs. It is the dynamics of competition, cooperation, and compromise among constituencies that ultimately shapes the decisions made by leaders inside and external to higher education.

Chapter 4—The Governor: The Key External Constituent

Perhaps the most important external constituent in influencing public higher education decisions is the governor. In most states, the governor seeks information from state agencies including higher education on short- and long-term plans and funding requirements, strategies to support state citizens, and mechanisms to improve state and local economic development. The governor's office also creates avenues to increase citizen participation in postsecondary education and demands justification to support additional state funding through annual and biennial budget processes.

The governor is an external authority that considers higher education needs while reacting to hundreds of competing statewide demands. It is the initial point where big-P politics (i.e., considering decisions based on party affiliations) comes into play in influencing the recommendations that are made. (While governors will rarely say they supported an initiative, budget, or program because of party politics, it is clear when decisions are connected to their public positions, statements, and actions.)

The big P and the little p of politics are present within the context of the governor's decisions and a major feature in how decisions are made. The SDMM's planning and assessment framework will incorporate the political considerations into alternatives addressing a specific scenario.

Chapter 5—The Legislature: The Final Arbiter of Funding

The legislature's primary task is to approve state-funding appropriations for all state agencies. Through various committees, it reviews funding requests and plans approved by the governor. The legislature has a number of other committees that look at nonbudgetary issues with implications on access, program expectations, citizen review, and much more. Needless to say, there is ongoing debate on how much funding is recommended for student access, program quality, employment opportunities, tuition cost limitations, etc. There is little financial emphasis on important issues like guns on campus or student conduct, yet they can rise to the top of political agendas. The immediacy (and visibility) of a particular issue such as a legislative priority to expand or limit gun-carrying rights to students has been a prominent issue in many states in recent years. Similarly increases in student drinking and rape have become a focus nationally as specific university or college examples become part of the national awareness and dialogue.

As in the case of the governor, the legislature is charged with recommending funding and taking other actions that affect public higher education and all state agencies. Perhaps even more apparent is the degree to which recommendations are based on competing political interests. As elected officials, legislators are making their decisions in many instances based on party loyalty. That is, they support a position that is forwarded by their leadership (local, state, or national) and is seen as consistent with party values. That is not to say that many legislators aren't supportive individually of a given initiative, but their allegiance to the party is a heavily weighted factor.

As in the case of the governor, the presence of big-P politics permeates decision-making and will be highlighted throughout the chapter. The planning and assessment framework of the SDMM will offer an outline through which the political variables can be considered.

Chapter 6—System and Governing Board Oversight

Public systems of higher education have generally had the responsibilities of oversight for resident access to a quality and affordable postsecondary education. The system is an administrative organization that supports an appointed governing board charged with the task of structuring the statewide goals, plans, and metrics for higher education. A primary responsibility is ensuring accountability in achieving goals by universities and community colleges that fall within the governing board's jurisdiction.

As can be imagined, the opportunities for multiple constituencies within the system to interact on the goal setting, planning, resource allocation, and achievement is literally unending in its scope and timing. Contention and compromise are continuing realities and necessities in assuring all voices are recognized. The board is at an intersection of the big-P politics in their connection to the legislature and governor (who is often the appointing authority of the board) while also working closely with the countless constituencies representing the little-p politics.

The use of the SDMM becomes of great value when comparing and contrasting the many internal and external demands that confront the board and its administrative arm, the system office.

Chapter 7—Institutional Leaders: Linking Local and System Goals

Institutional presidents, chancellors, and their leadership teams are expected to incorporate their "share" of the system-level goals and create plans, budgets, anticipated outcomes, and accountability reports in meeting statewide or system goals. As a consequence, the institutional leadership should consistently be in communications with key constituencies such as students, faculty, and system leaders in their efforts to address their concerns. The interaction of constituencies at an institutional level may be as important in the points of contention and compromise within the context of the little-p politics as the eventual debate that is taken from the institution to the system and the public. There should be a connection of the substance of political debates and decisions occurring internally with those happening outside of higher education

Institutional leaders act as lynchpins between their institution and the governor's office, system office, governing board, legislative leaders, legislative committees, internal constituencies like the students and faculty, and many more entities. The obvious outcome is the necessity to balance the competing demands in as transparent, equitable, and comprehensive manner as possible.

The role of institutional leaders will be explored in the context of leading in a highly dynamic and, at times, a charged environment. The use of the SDMM and specifically planning and assessment framework in maximizing the opportunities for fair treatment, for all will become increasingly apparent.

Chapter 8—Students as Consumers Individually and Collectively

Students are the recipients of a public postsecondary education. Individually and as a group they have the most to lose and gain when decisions are made. Students are generally organized through their own government and related committees. Their government works within the institution, which gives them a number of avenues to communicate their concerns, expectations and, even at times, demands. While student organizations are primarily for internal purposes, like representation through student government, they also can take on active roles in communicating with the local community, governor's office, and the legislature.

The chapter will review their roles and connections with other constituencies and see how they are integrated into the overall decision-making process. There are times when their agenda is embraced and others when it is not depending on the internal and external conditions of the times. As in other chapters, the SDMM will offer alternative solutions that respond to a scenario with implications for students and other constituencies

Chapter 9—Faculty: Individual and Collective Value to Higher Education

Each faculty member represents the primary resource to support the institutional goals of teaching, research/discovery, and service. They interact with students, departmental and college leaders, the public, the board, legislators, accrediting agencies, their colleagues, and others in their multidimensional roles. They are often viewed with high regard as teacher but not acknowledged in a way they feel recognizes their value. Over the years, as state funding has declined, faculty compensation has not kept pace with the expectations of faculty, often relative to peers in other institutions. As the frustration over compensation has grown, student faculty ratios have increased, and demands for accountability have risen, within an environment expecting more service and discovery. The faculty has been taking more aggressive positions on compensation and teaching given the sense of lack of support from internal and external leaders. The perception or reality of a lack of support have become a continuing point of dissent and debate.

A scenario highlighting a number of factors affecting higher education and faculty will be presented with alternative solutions being developed through the planning and assessment framework (of the SDMM).

Chapter 10—Internal Influences on Decisions (Cross-Cutting Issues)

The questions are often raised regarding the implications of key issues within systems and institutions that affect and are affected by internal constituencies. The issues of tuition increases and student access, salary adjustments for faculty and competitiveness with peer institutions, and program quality represent often contentious points for debate. Also, graduation rates and recruitment for jobs, state-funding support as compared to student costs, financial aid capacity, guns and safety on campus, and equity by race, religion, and gender, among others, are all hot-button issues that imply different meanings to different constituencies.

The chapter will identify how the primary constituencies of students, faculty, staff, and leadership are organized to represent their priorities and work with one another to communicate those priorities. There are many entities or bodies that represent various interest groups—student government and numerous related committees, faculty unions, faculty committees, multiple organizational committees dealing with budget, compensation, facilities, student conduct, strategic planning initiatives, etc., each with representation of multiple constituencies. It is this chapter, that may best reflect the little-p politics in the sheer magnitude of internal interest groups that interact with one another.

A scenario identifying one key issue that affects all constituencies will be filtered through the planning and assessment framework and alternative solutions created for leadership consideration.

Chapter 11—External Influences on Internal Decisions

Groups external to system and institutions of public higher education have interests in what public higher education offers to a states citizenry, when it is offered and at what cost. They are also interested in how programs are developed, presented, and assessed. What is the quality of academic programs (based on agreed-upon standards)? Are entry and retention guidelines consistent with student access goals? Does graduation lead to a job? Are student costs competitive with peer institutions (what factors determine a peer institution)? And many more.

The federal government through student financial aid, extensive research funding, and multiple reporting requirements on access, conduct, safety, facilities, and quality has a key role in how higher education administers its programs. Needless to say, the availability of funding influences how and what programs are developed and offered.

Accrediting agencies compare academic and university-wide programs to various standards and offer critical analysis of those areas under review. Their recommendations have major impacts on what and how programs are structured.

The National Collegiate Athletic Association has been increasing its oversight role in recent years. NCAA requirements have been debated actively as new instances of infractions have appeared. The expectations for academic improvement, oversight of the sexual conduct of athletic programs, financial oversight and control, and equity in men's and women's athletic funding create major efforts in monitoring, controlling, and reporting raw data and outcomes

A scenario will be offered highlighting one of the issues driven by external constituencies. In this case, the executive planning and budget office will be the focus with the implications of its requirements assessed through the planning assessment framework of the SDMM.

Chapter 12—Application of the Strategic Decision-Making Model

Higher education is subject to many influences both internally within each institution and from forces outside the institution. It is necessary to develop mechanisms to identify the influences whether they are negative, positive, or neutral. In reality they can affect how, what, and when decisions are made. The focus of this book is on the constituents and how they are often forced to react to one another's agendas in realizing their own priorities. The influences are defined as political, first as typically portrayed within legislative and executive branch politics/elections, and second as suggested through the interactions of constituencies seeking their share of support from their own leaders. While party politics is more visible and apparent at each level of government constituency politics is as much a contributor to decisions that eventually shape higher education programs and outcomes.

The chapter will have an extended and complex scenario that will be reviewed through the six components of the SDMM. The interaction of **strategic thinking** with **strategic planning, sufficient accurate and timely information, future scanning,** and the **planning and assessment framework (P and A framework)** all in a **transparent** environment represent what is necessary for a leader to make good choices. The application of all six components of the SDMM offers a resource that can view and filter information that is objective, subjective, political, apolitical, data driven, historical, and even disruptive.

Constituencies, Politics, and Influence

To this point and moving forward it will be clear that use of the term *politics* encompasses much more than the competition between two or three major political parties seeking to gain advantages in respective local, state, and national jurisdictions. While the ultimate approval of solutions for funding (state appropriation) or program support may be done through executive and legislative mandates, the interaction of interest groups (constituencies) feeding their demands into the many-layered bureaucratic processes is of great significance. The power of constituencies, fighting for their share of diminished resources to cover years of strong or limited support for priorities and as filtered through many levels of government, cannot be denied.

It is the debate at each level of government on taxes, public responsibility for an educated citizenry, safe communities, support for the needy, maintenance of roads, national security, etc., that eventually coalesces around ideas and solutions to meet societies' highest priorities. It is the hallmark of American government that decisions are made based on wide ranging public input in many different forums, both public and private. Elected and appointed representatives make choices based their interpretation of the public's beliefs and priorities. The choices they make will often be at odds with some segment of the electorate they represent and, as a consequence, keep differences of opinion continuously in the public arena.

It is the continuing approval or disapproval by the public that determines the fate of decision makers (elected and administrative) to represent public interests. Disapproval generally represents dissent with the actions or beliefs of those in a position to make final decisions. Disapproval may translate into a loss of authority to make decisions on behalf of the public. Whether the public approves or disapproves of elected or administrative officials, they have the means to modify elected oversight through voicing their opinion at the polls.

Attempting to influence one person or interest group in the direction of another is generally not a simple understanding between two parties on a given issue. It is rather a complex, multifactored compromise built on years of agreement and disagreement on many issues of mutual concern. The extent of influence varies based on the interacting expectations of multiple constituencies and the relative "value" of the issues they are fighting for (or against). Decisions made by leaders represent an intricate hybrid conclusion considering current input, ideological assumptions, past priorities, assessment of risks and rewards, and probable outcomes. Even the most simplistic and obvious choices are likely based on historical precedent, ideological philosophy, and the inputs of the most powerful constituencies at the time.

Political activity is not only the most visible manifestation of political parties but encompasses constituent interactions contributing to the decisions made by their representatives. Politics is found in legislative and organizational public hearings and forums and individual meetings between constituent and political or administrative representatives. It is also found at administrative and constituent leadership meetings, forums for organizational discussions and debates, meetings held in private settings without public representation, meetings including political leaders only, and various other avenues to communicate issues of importance to competing constituencies and their respective internal and external leaders.

Through the application of the SDMM, it is possible to assess multiple variables that can contribute to determining why, how, and what decisions are made by leaders. Even in the most complex environments of constituent dissonance and political distress, it is possible to drive toward logic that makes sense based on historical realities, current conditions, and future expectations. Well-informed decisions can be made when there is the requisite planning and assessment encompassing the goals of all constituencies. Strategic thinking and planning are the foundation of a decision-making process that is built on transparency and communications. While decisions are not always popular, they will benefit from greater legitimacy and support when they are made within the parameters of a comprehensive and thoughtfully constructed process.

Assessing What Influences Constituencies: Applying the Strategic Decision-Making Model

INTERACTIONS AMONG COMPETING and cooperating constituencies create a dynamic of uncertainty, tension, and instability. The uncertainty is driven by the unknown reactions of key actors, perceptions of conflict, and inability to gain support for key initiatives. The uncertainty raises a need to build new or enhanced avenues of communication that may or may not help gain a positive outcome. At best, increasing communications may gain some support and limit uncertainty. At worst, if there is no uncertainty in the decision maker's position (e.g., they don't support constituent priorities), then there is little room for further cooperation and compromise.

Tension is a byproduct of uncertainty and is magnified by the degree to which cooperation is limited. Limiting tension can only come about if there is greater certainty that constituent initiatives are being accepted by decision makers. Seeking to force interactions among constituencies can increase tension as competition escalates and differences are magnified.

Instability comes from a lack of support by decision makers of constituency's priorities. Lack of support drives constituencies to seek alternative paths to gain some positive visibility and ideally approval. Different paths may include campaigning against other constituency positions or realigning your priorities to better fit the direction of leadership. It may also, even more dramatically, include attacking leadership decisions publicly as a means to leverage more acceptable outcomes. The objective to limit instability has inherent risks if there is a sense that only aggressive actions against other constituencies or leadership is necessary.

Each of the dynamics can be at least partially avoided with thoughtful planning that is strategic, well-communicated, comprehensive, and timely. It must be constructed to give leaders the confidence that it has pursued all variables that will contribute to the best decision possible. The application of the SDMM provides a framework that can reduce uncertainty experienced in less comprehensive processes, reduce tension associated with plans and actions that are not reflective of all viable options, and eliminate instability that is typical of processes that don't consider constituency expectations and the implications of leadership recommendations on those constituencies.

The more accurate information a decision maker is armed with when negotiating with multiple constituencies, the greater the opportunity to be successful in a highly competitive environment. Success can be measured based on the degree to which goals are achieved, which in many instances is a willingness to accept compromise. If the compromise moves the programs toward greater success, even if not realizing the primary goal fully, it does legitimize the program and resources necessary to keep it viable. The willingness to find common ground also gives all constituencies a sense that dialogue, debate, and even disagreement can bear positive outcomes. Ultimately, it suggests that dialogue and negotiations in the future can begin where the prior ones ended.

The SDMM will be interwoven into the discussion to provide points of reference for leaders. The SDMM is comprised of six key components:

1. Strategic thinking
2. Information and data analyses
3. Future scanning nationally and globally
4. Strategic planning
5. Transparency
6. Planning and assessment framework

Strategic Decision-Making Model: Components for Success

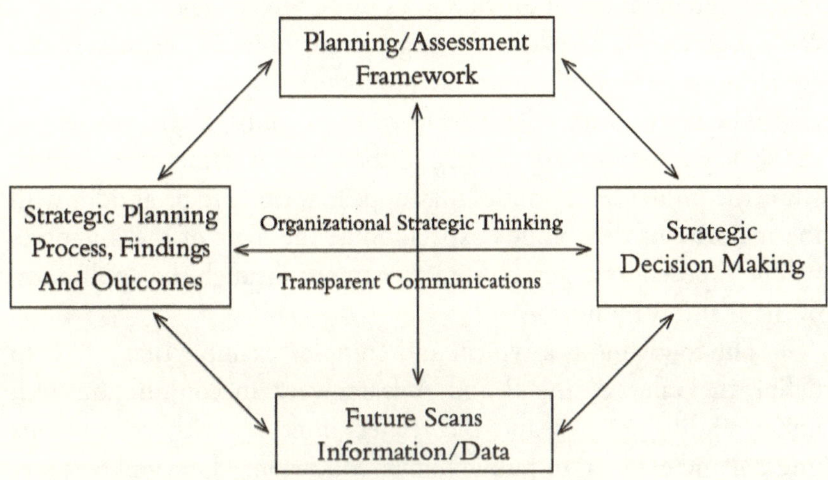

Source: *Navigating Through Turbulent Times: Applying a System and University Decision Making Model* (Anderes, 2015)

It is hoped that informed leaders will be **thinking strategically** and will consider all **information resources** strategically with close attention to global events and **future potentials**. It is assumed some form of comprehensive **strategic planning process** will be used within the context of an organization that embraces daily decisions framed through **transparency of thought and action**. If those assumptions are achieved, then the **planning and assessment framework (P and A framework)** will prompt leaders to all relevant options and derive solutions that are as fully informed as they can be.

If leaders are fully informed, then their chances of reaching desired goals and outcomes will be enhanced.

The P and A framework is a tool to examine and assess information used by leaders to provide alternatives for their consideration. It will be applied in this book in ten different scenarios to guide readers understanding of how alternative solutions are constructed. It does not necessarily produce a final decision but does give thoughtful options for leaders to incorporate into larger macro planning process.

How does the planning and assessment framework relate to a book on politics and political influence? As political activities and related outcomes are often viewed as more subjective in nature, how can a framework based on driving toward objective responses and conclusions be logically connected to a meaningful end?

The connection will arise from the quality of the answers to the six key questions that undergird the P and A framework. That is, while the influence of politics may appear at times to be at odds with the majority of the public's expectations, the logic of the outcomes will be exposed by a step by step assessment through the application of the P and A framework.

The following is a typical and complex example that will help define the value of the P and A framework in conjunction with understanding politics and the related interplay with constituents internal and external to public higher education. There will be a scenario that provides background on issues confronting public higher education that are typical of what has been prevalent in recent years. The planning and assessment framework of the SDMM will act as a filter to ask and answer key questions raised by the scenario. There will then be alternative solutions that offer differing rationale a leader might consider in addressing the primary points raised in the scenario. There are three alternatives assuming that decisions will be made on the basis of circumstances that may differ by state and system of higher education. The differences will render variations in how leaders may react to the same scenario.

(The P and A framework will be the primary tool to guide leaders through assessment of issues and problems posed in nine separate scenarios as expressed through in chapters 1 and 4-11. The full six components of the SDMM including the P and A framework will be used in the final chapter to highlight interactive connections of the model in a more complex scenario. It is recognized that the only way of making well informed decisions is through the use of the full model. However, the scenarios leading up to chapter 12 are filtered through the P and A framework to focus on the questions surrounding the implications of constituency politics under specific conditions. As stated at the outset of the book, using the full model to review each chapter and constituency would lose its value in the amount of detail and time to construct a complete analysis.)

Planning and Assessment Framework: Multivariable Analysis of Financial, Programmatic, and Demographic Factors Shaping Constituent Positions and Leadership Decisions

Applying the Planning and Assessment Framework

Scenario

Higher education leaders were confronted with a drop in state-funding support of 7% while coming off a year of limited increases of tuition—2% for state residents and 10% for nonresidents. The governor and legislature were offering greater flexibility in the use of the funds but based on conditions that there would be a measurable increase in students attaining jobs following graduation and that graduation would be on a quicker path (from 5.5 years to 4.5 years for bachelor's degrees). Students argued for more financial aid and no tuition increases. Faculty and staff sought 15% increases in compensation spread over a three-year period. The state economy was stable but with little growth expected in state revenues and a continuing emphasis on reducing tax rates.

The interaction between constituencies was respectful but with increasing frustration based on the perception that each did not understand the others' problems. Students felt they paid too much with relatively no increases in value. The faculty felt they were not appreciated and were not competitive with national peers in compensation. Higher education administration leaders were attempting to balance very little positive news on more flexible use of fewer funds with the reality that there would be reductions to various programs and services. System and institutional leaders would argue eloquently for new funds (or smaller reductions) as a show of support for faculty and staff, but the arguments would be inconsequential in gaining added support. Embedded within all the issues under review were a history of distrust by faculty for leadership support, a series of state reductions in funding for public higher education, students' concern for a lack of representation in institutional decision-making on issues they confront, and legislative skepticism about public higher education justifications for funding (i.e., even a sense that higher education provides dishonest information).

There are many other considerations that cross constituent lines, but we will keep the example, although complex, as clear as possible as we apply the P and A framework. The framework consists of six primary questions (and multiple subsets of questions) that help guide higher education leaders. The system and university chancellors or presidents can individually and collectively create responses to the questions that become the basis for compromise and final positions on key issues. It is expected that the same questions are pursued with faculty, staff, and students as input for planning consideration and as precedent to any final decisions made by higher education leaders. Ultimately, a comprehensive data and information base representing all constituency thoughts and recommendations is made available as a resource to better understand the trail of decisions from a point of initiation to final approvals by the state/system board.

The Planning and Assessment Framework

1. What is the problem? What creates instability? Is there
   agreement on the problem?

The defining problem in this scenario is the diminishing state resources necessary to successfully maintain student, faculty, and staff programs and services. The problem is not disputed by the internal constituencies. It is the lack of resources that drives a host of other issues felt, to varying degrees by the students, faculty, and staff. The loss of resources stimulates the competition among all parties interested in retaining and growing their programs and financial base.

The key external constituents see the issues differently from higher education. The governor is content with the budget recommended to the legislature. The legislature seeks to limit increases in statewide taxes, and as a consequence, reduced funding for many state programs actually becomes a goal. The distribution of the cuts among agencies is often disputed, but the majority of legislators must agree on final appropriations. When legislators disagree with the preliminary appropriation and specific program reductions, it provides an opportunity for constituencies to argue publicly for their programs. The public is not always supportive of higher education, however, so arguments will be heard both embracing and opposing program and funding requests.

Constituent politics is relatively straightforward, the system and institutional leaders will argue to the governor and legislature for greater funding based on their original budget requests. The governor may fight to have funding added back if the legislature makes cuts more deeply than recommended by the governor.

Ultimately, students, faculty, and higher education leaders will seek added funds through legislative forums (appropriation and higher education related committees and hearings). They will also spend a substantial time lobbying key legislators about their programs' value to various districts and the state as a whole.

At this point in defining the problem, the politics of the overall environment appears simple and even unidimensional. The complexity of the problem runs far deeper, however. Students will be arguing amongst themselves, with institutional leaders and system decision makers when justifying their priority positions. Faculty will be debating courses of action within their own committees, departments, and colleges; arguing with administrative leadership; and offering alternative solutions to anyone who will listen. Students and faculty will bring their concerns directly to the legislature particularly if they feel institutional leaders are ignoring their needs.

The complexity of constituent competition grows as the implications of reduced funding impacts more constituents and as the support by the governor and legislature goes into a downward spiral. The historical commitment by the external constituents to higher education drives a wedge of discontent among all and exacerbates the competition for what remains. That tension can lead to some difficulties in finding common ground and compromise positions. Instability is inevitable.

(Note: We have discussed the problem at a very general level without moving into the more detailed expectations of higher education constituencies. As the examination dives deeper into the issues of the politics of competition and compromise, the differences and divisions become even more evident. The researchers and planners providing the analytical support responding to the P and A questions to various leaders and committees will look into the question in much greater depth.)

2. What examples contribute to the problem? What is the
   magnitude of the problem?

The key problem is the lack of resources available to the state. The most obvious sources of funding loss are state revenues in the form of personal income tax and state sales taxes. The losses have come about due to intentional reductions in tax rates and losses related to no growth in sales or personal income. The great recession clearly impacted revenue losses by driving fewer purchases and limiting or even reducing personal income (through the loss of jobs contributing to taxes and reduced compensation to those who maintained some level of employment). While sales taxes typically rebound following recessions the commitment to limited personal tax continues in many states.

The lack of state resources creates dissent among constituencies in the general goals of the state, systems, and institutions as a logical outcome in the variance of respective priorities. That is, faculty seek increased compensation, students expect limited tuition growth and increased financial aid, and system leaders make requests that respond to statewide priorities but not necessarily each institution's priorities. While there may be some marginal improvements such as the students not absorbing large increases in tuition or faculty receiving some compensation increase the lessening of state funds forces each constituency to develop strategies that will maximize their results while reducing the opportunities for others. Often the competition for scarce resources is divisive and long-lasting. The greater the magnitude of reductions in state funds the greater the uncertainty in their capacity to meet primary goals.

3. What is the origin of the current examples of the problem? What caused the problem?

The origin of reductions in resources is simply a lack of funding driven through various taxes (sales and personal income, primarily) at the state level to allocate to various state agencies. Arguments to grow agency funding revolve around how to increase taxes or how agencies can justify a greater share of existing revenues. The arguments to grow or not to grow the tax base are as political in nature as any in government. The competition for scarce revenues is even more political. Understanding the position of many constituencies within and external to higher education is important in building a framework of determining who is competing and to what end.

Understanding the derivation of problems contributing to decline provides a point of departure in not only assessing what happened and why but also establishing alternative pathways to better follow in the future.

The value of an in-depth inventory and assessment of what caused the key problems is to offer answers to current concerns. If problems and their causes are adequately documented in forward looking planning, it reduces the likelihood of future uncertainty and interaction among constituencies. In this instance the loss of state funds spawns multiple problems that can be isolated with the components of the SDMM. The irony of being successful in the future is the necessity to apply what has been learned from the past. Thus, understanding the origin of problems creating uncertainty and instability is critical.

4. Is there a historical precedent for the problem? Does the
   precedent connect with current issues?

Most states in the last ten to fifteen years have realized reduced revenues as consequence of the financial recession felt globally. Even before the recession, many states had been moving toward reducing state taxes and overall governmental costs. There had been growing concern by some that government was growing too big and wasn't accountable to the people. The outcome has been continuing arguments between states and their constituencies including higher education about the inability to provide the programs and services that the public desires. To date, the supporters of small government and reduced taxes have prevailed nationally and to an even larger degree at the state level. What the future holds is relatively clear, that federal and state resources will focus on safety, health issues, and entitlements, and even less funding will be available for discretionary programs like higher education. As a consequence, there will be more competition and a greater burden of resourcefulness placed on the individual. As government gets out of the business of supporting various social, educational, welfare, and other programs, it is up to individuals to go with less or find other costlier means to continue services they feel are necessary.

5. Which constituencies are most affected? Do all constituencies feel there is a problem? What is the relative stake of each?

In higher education, institutions, systems, students, faculty, staff, etc., are all affected in some manner when funding is reduced. As suggested in the conditions of our original problem the faculty felt they were not adequately compensated, students felt the value of the education was diminished, and higher education leaders felt they could not provide the quantity and quality programs and services that state citizens deserved or wanted. The public felt they were not getting the value they expected from their higher education system—yet weren't willing to address the drop in state funding as a major reason.

All constituencies agreed there is a problem and generally each felt they were most disadvantaged. The feelings of being uncertain of how they would fare in competition meant that they all had something at stake and more specifically something to lose.

Leaders would look at solutions that helped each constituency continue to receive and provide programming that was viable and of sufficient quality to be respected internally and externally. It would mean that faculty would receive reduced compensation increases, students would pay a higher tuition and receive marginal increase in technology and classroom services, and leaders would have to balance the needs of constituencies through compromise and offer hope for a brighter future. Any promises for the future would depend on additional political support, sufficient state resources, and a general acceptance that higher education as a state priority should be elevated.

6. Provide alternatives or actions on how to strategically prepare for and address similar examples in the future (specify timeline, outcomes, and metrics).

There are a number of alternatives (solutions) that should address the specific issues raised in this scenario. The intersection of external politics and internal constituent expectations or demands should be a primary focus of higher education decision makers. The intersection or overlap does occur regularly when statewide funding, planning, and policy issues have implications for public higher education programs. In this scenario, there are numerous points of intersection that force higher education leaders to determine how best to develop and market their strategies to the external parities (the governor and legislature primarily).

In this scenario and all others, at some predetermined point near the completion of the internal strategic planning processes, after considering strengths and weaknesses of the primary alternatives, leaders should do a final filtering of solutions and make their choices. A summary of choices should include at least one alternative with the implications of actions that best meet the agreed-upon goals of public higher education as envisioned by system and institutional leaders. Ideally, the alternative will have considered all constituent concerns (i.e., internal and external constituencies) and offer a plan that recognizes the value of each constituency whether their recommendations were supported or not. It can't be emphasized too much that as leaders make decisions they should be assessing how and why the governor and legislature will react to higher education plans and budget. If there is an understanding of how external constituencies will respond to a given set of assumptions, strategies, plans, and funding needs, then internal leaders can be better prepared to defend their decisions.

The following are three simple alternatives addressing the issues of this scenario with varying degrees of impact on the respective priorities of each constituency. The politics shape the perceptions of internal constituent support for each alternative and influences the degrees of dissent. The depth of dissent will have implications on both the immediate and longer-term relationships and in turn influence how leaders make decisions. Ultimately, the acceptance of decisions by all constituencies will be based on success as defined by those who benefit the most or the least when decisions are made. How success is defined at the outset of planning and how that changes when solutions are implemented represents a critical stage in the acceptance of decisions by constituencies. The degree to which the competition among constituencies can lead to compromises of some benefit to all will determine immediate and long-term relationships.

As we move into considering potential alternatives, let's restate the key conditions of the overall scenario.

- There have been a number of years where state funding has been reduced. The prolonged nature of reduced state funding has eliminated most opportunities for budget cutting short of program elimination.
- The state presents a goal to reduce taxes for residents. A reduction of taxes will mean a loss in revenues for state agencies.
- Higher education will lose an additional 7% of state funds in the upcoming year thus compounding historical losses.
- Tuition will increase 2% for resident students and 10% for nonresident students. While the increase is relatively minor for state students, they are working with substantial increases from prior years.
- The governor promises increased flexibility in the use of state funds where job attainment is increased and graduation rates are increased.
- Students seek no tuition increase and increased financial aid.
- The faculty is requesting a 15% compensation increase over a three-year period.
- Seeds of distrust:

  1. Students see no value in their paying greater tuition for no new programs or services.
  2. Faculty feel underappreciated within the state and relative to peer institutions.
  3. The legislature is skeptical of higher education's use of state funds. They require accountability for the use of state and student generated funds but with limited incentives for efficiency or effectiveness.

4. Higher education leadership provides substantial amounts of objective data supporting requests but realizes that the legislature collectively views higher education as discretionary and as such not a priority.

Alternatives

Alternative 1: Assuming a reduction of 3% (as opposed to the 7% recommendation) in state-funding support, higher education leaders will seek increased tuition rates, limit faculty compensation increases, and request increased flexibility in administering programs from the executive and legislative branches. (The alternative considers less of a reduction in state funds as one strategy to lobby with the governor and legislature. The intent is to shift attention to a more acceptable outcome and be prepared to justify its value.)

The leaders will work with students and faculty on recognizing opportunities in the future to limit tuition rate increases and increase faculty compensation. The outcomes will be based on compromise on both immediate and long-term agreements between constituencies. Leadership will also hopefully be able to identify other new sources of revenue to fill the gap left by state funds.

Students will argue they are receiving no tangible benefit for paying higher costs. They will look at comparisons of their tuition and fees relative to peer institutions, and if they are higher, they will seek some reversal of institutional decisions. There is potential for heavy lobbying within the institution, in the community, and with the governor and legislature.

Faculty may be happy with even limited increases, but that is likely only if there are promises for future compensation growth. There will be some turmoil in looking down the road and assessing whether or not instructional programs will have to be cut. The loss of state funds may dictate program reductions.

System and institutional leadership will have to redefine plans that promise growth based on revenue projections that can't be realized. The planning must be based on as accurate a sense of growth in enrollments, tuition, and state revenues as possible, even to the extent of reducing existing projections. The outcome of new estimates may create significant campus and state distress particularly if no new revenues are identified. If it is felt that student tuition cannot be grown to offset state losses, then it becomes necessary to consider reductions to existing programs. The use of SDMM components such as strategic planning processes and the planning and assessment framework will be critical in attaining the best information possible.

Alternative 2: Assuming there is no reduction in state funding (as opposed to the governor's 7%) support, higher education leaders will ask faculty to increase their class workloads to reduce the number of faculty on payroll. (This alternative, while not expected to gain support from external constituencies, is a means of reflecting to all internal constituencies that leaderships support for the higher education programs as they currently exist.)

They will seek added funds from the state but in a relatively minimal fashion realizing all agencies are in a similar position. The faculty will receive a limited increase in salary. The leaders will propose an increase in nonresident and international students (at increased tuition rates) with no growth in resident students for two years. The continuing resident students will not be subject to an increase in tuition rates for two years. The system and institutional leaders must actively lobby the executive and legislative branches to assure that resident students are not being disenfranchised in attaining their education. There will also be a greater effort in gain new funds through entrepreneurial means and shifting some state costs to local or self-supporting activities.

The dependence in gaining new funds from the state should be considered as an opportunity that is not likely to occur. The increase in tuition from nonresident students is a typical approach to ensuring access to students who are residents. However, there must be well-grounded estimates on the implications of increasing tuition for nonresident and international students. Increasing tuition will be of limited benefit if the enrollments drop in response to the increases.

Alternative 2 is a best-case option that, while it is unlikely, provides planners and leaders with thoughtful counterpoints to alternative 1 and as we will see alternative 3. Planning should be about exploring multiple directions so that all constituencies will have a sense of how leaders will be supportive under differing circumstances. In alternative 2, they see that their programs are considered of value and should be heartened as they look to more positive times.

As in the case of alternative 1, there must be a systematic planning assessment (SDMM) that looks closely at enrollments, state revenues/appropriations, tuition resources, etc., to ensure funding estimates for upcoming years are more conditioned to lowered expectations. The model can also put an emphasis through the strategic planning efforts to place a high priority on identifying new sources of funding.

Alternative 3: Assuming a reduction of 8% in funding the system, board members and institutional leaders will actively lobby to more aggressively make the state aware of what will be lost if the recommendations are approved. (In this alternative, the actual reduction is greater than laid out by the governor. It is being considered to be sure that institutions are preparing for outcomes that will reduce many programs and is the most realistic of the three alternatives.)

They will begin public dialogue by looking at the implications of an 8% cut along with the accumulation of reductions in recent years. Students will have to pay a higher tuition to help offset the losses. Compensation increase for faculty will be deferred into future years. The goal will be clarified to the public upon further erosion in quality and access. The politics will be focused on down in the trenches competition in gaining a larger share of the funding even at the cost of other state agencies. Legislators, particularly in college towns or jurisdictions, will be singled out if they support the reduction or other issues working against higher education. Students and faculty will be asked to work closely in communicating a common theme of distress on a number of levels.

Public lobbying must begin as soon as the message of downsizing is clear and communicated internally. The planning that supports the public communications must incorporate the true extent of the drop in state funds on all institutional programs and services.

The students will be the only certain resource for added funding and, as a consequence, will be questioning the value of their education given potential losses in instructional options (if programs are reduced). They will likely be even more vocal about their position in the decisions and be even more active in their lobbying with the community, the governor, and the legislature. The system and institutional leadership will have to offer some incentives to students that will give them a sense that their arguments ae being heard.

Faculty will be equally as distressed when their expectations for a compensation increase are deferred. They will also create avenues to lobby in the institution for their share of funding. The question becomes what is their share of resources in a diminished environment? The power of the faculty to question leadership decisions can't be underplayed, and in the end, they will be seeking some incentives to support leadership plans.

The identification of new fund sources becomes even more critical in this scenario, and as such, there should be incentives offered to faculty and others that can shift some state funding to grants, download state costs to self-supporting programs where practical, and create more entrepreneurial, private enterprises aligned with a campus that can infuse revenues.

The system and institutional leadership, as in alternatives 1 and 2, must reassess their plans for the short-term and long-term future. The planning assessment is even more critical given there will be losses in state funding and the potential for real reductions to programs, faculty, and staff. Again, the SDMM is a necessary tool for the system and institution to arrive at a realistic view of program, financial, and enrollment growth or decline moving into the future.

Choosing an Alternative: Gauging Political Reaction

Each alternative has value relative to system and institutional goals and priorities but will have very different implications for each constituency. The presence of political competition both internally (among constituencies) and externally (governor and legislature) for scarce resources is significant. The governor and legislature aren't looking to provide new resources to most state agencies, and within higher education, there are multiple priorities supported by numerous constituencies that are vying for at least some relevance. The ability to reach consensus or compromise is built around many factors which will change from year to year. Factors such as funding, program priorities, taxing policies, external political infighting, and public sentiment can contribute to an unsettled environment for negotiating. The greater the losses in funding and increases in competition, the greater the potential for dissonance among competitors. Alternative 3 reflects the direction with the greatest risk to constituencies. Competition would be more intense for fewer resources and chances for compromise greatly reduced. There would still be competition under the conditions in alternatives 1 and 2 but potentially with fewer volatile interactions.

There is general agreement that the primary problem is diminished state resources. The cuts in the state funding are a catalyst for competition between constituencies. The loss of state funds in turn leads to options of seeking other funding sources, reducing program costs, and increasing existing sources of funding, like tuition funds. The options ramp up the anxiety and intensity in competition.

All the constituencies are affected and realize that their futures are at stake if not in the next year, then potentially in the future, hence the extreme amount of competition and political interaction.

Regardless of the alternative chosen and interaction among constituencies, higher education leaders will have to gauge the capacity of the governor and legislature to change their positions. The willingness of the executive and legislative branches to add and subtract programs and services in response to higher education recommendations is, at best, limited. Leaders will have to work with students and faculty on building a united front. They must give the appearance to the public that any reductions will have direct consequences on student access, program quality, and the ability of institutions to meet basic state expectations. Students and their families must feel threatened in that they may not get access to critical degree programs, and they will be unable to gain the qualifications necessary to successfully compete in the marketplace.

Alternatives 1-3 represent solutions that affect each constituency differently. When one benefits from a decision, another may be harmed. The decision to address higher faculty compensation may require added tuition, the loss in state funding may require a limitation in enrollment growth, limiting tuition growth may impact funding for new faculty programming, and the multiple implications of change on constituencies is significant.

Constituent expectations for increased compensation, greater flexibility, and limited tuition increases all demand resources that external constituents (state and federal government) are unable or willing to provide. The politics then breaks down into one-on-one conversations among internal constituents and external parties, multiple legislative forums to air complaints, and higher education committees and meetings offering the public the perspective of how they will be negatively affected into the future. The intention of higher education leaders is to find reasonable compromises that their constituents will find acceptable and that maintain program momentum. The intention of faculty and staff is to realize an increase in support or at least a minor share of the reduction. Legislators want to limit any additions that increase their projected expenditures. Perhaps as importantly they don't want to make exceptions that may lead to other constituencies and state agencies becoming emboldened.

Connecting the Alternatives and SDMM

Most importantly while there are no good alternatives in dealing with financial decline, there must be a process as envisioned through the SDMM that can identify key issues, understand their relative historical, current, and future values, and create solutions that represent the best outcomes for all. All constituencies will demand data, expect opportunities for debate, consistent communications, and transparent rationale for change particularly as it may negatively affect them.

The alternatives provide examples of how to react to a given scenario within the context of multiple constituent expectations. Their expectations should be focused through the planning and assessment framework. Consistency in assessment of the issues, key factors of influence, and internal and external politics, surrounding leader's decisions must be clear and transparent to all.

Chapter 2 will define politics while chapter 3 will define constituency and both will provide context for scenarios in the remaining chapters. You will be able to more fully assess the pressures of competition, cooperation, and compromise within the interactions of internal and external constituencies.

What Is Politics and How Does It Influence Decision-Making?

IT IS IMPORTANT to define the term *politics* to understand its meaning on multiple levels. This book uses more than one definition to clarify key relationships within and outside of higher education. Most everyone has their version of what politics means. However, it can be different if the perspective is of an individual or a group or even from a societal level. That is, politics are seen as personal, where an individual views their own political understanding of how and why decisions are made.

Politics can also be viewed from the broader local, state, or national level of competition between political parties. As an example, should taxes be raised nationally or reduced to achieve governmental goals? Democrats feel differently about taxation than Republicans generally. There are significant divides on how big the federal government is in its reach into American lives and its cost. The question is often raised as to what the role of the federal government should be versus state government in the provision of services to its citizens. The basic differences can stimulate intense debates and, as seen in recent years, be a catalyst for incivility between parties on many key issues. It is the differences that highlight the continuing competition at national and state levels and often is felt at the more local levels of government.

There is an even larger sense of politics when considered at a societal level. The societal level extends globally and reflects arguments addressing conditions of hunger, climate change, military action, immigration, or poverty, to name just a few. There are wide differences that exist within the United States between political parties on policies and oversight for immigration. Those same differences exist within many countries internationally and the ability to find national or international solutions or even begrudging compromise is nearly nonexistent.

The following formal definitions capture that general range of politics depending on one's perspective.

Definitions of Politics

Merriam-Webster:

1. The art or science concerned with guiding or influencing governmental policy.
2. Competition between competing interest groups or individuals for power and leadership
3. The political opinions or sympathies of a person.
4. The total complex of relations between people living in society.

Source: *Merriam-Webster* online dictionary, retrieved November 2016

The Free Dictionary:

1. The art or science of government or governing, especially the governing of a political entity, such as a nation, and the administration and control of its internal and external affairs.
2. Intrigue or maneuvering within a political unit or a group in order to gain control of power.

3.   The often internally conflicting interrelationships among people in society.

Source: The Free Dictionary online dictionary, retrieved November 2016

Interpreting the Definitions

Much can be taken from the definitions. There is an emphasis on variety of areas including the following: influencing public policy, control from the internal and external perspective, competition among interest groups, intrigue and conflict of relationships, and opinions ranging from an individual to societal issues of concern. It is relatively easy to translate the meaning of politics to interactions and relationships occurring at the federal and state levels to the interactions at the inner and inter institutional and system levels in public higher education. The debate by the students and institutional leadership regarding increasing financial aid or offering more classes is the interrelationship of two constituencies competing for scarce resources. The discussions by faculty and their leadership regarding the quality of programs or receiving additional compensation represent constituent competition for scarce resources. There are multiple levels of debate and competition beginning with constituencies in an institution and decisions made by institutional leaders. Institutional plans are then debated at the system level and consolidated in a modified form to submit externally to the governor and legislature. The system plans and requests representing the institutions compete with other state agency plans, external state-level priorities, and scarce resources. They are further modified and funding-appropriated as an outcome of public reviews by the governor and legislature.

In chapter 1, politics was identified as either internal, as competition among higher education constituencies, or external, as characterized by political entities such as the governor and legislature. In taking this analogy, one step further, external politics was large-P politics focusing on the priorities, activities, competition, and outcomes of political parties, such as Democrats, Republicans, and independents. Small-p politics would focus on constituencies within public higher education like students, faculty, academic and administrative staff, leadership, etc., and the completion for priority program support among those constituencies. (Throughout this book, internal politics is synonymous with little-p politics and external politics is synonymous with big-P politics.)

Merriam-Webster suggests that politics is "wining and holding control in government" while the Free Dictionary defines *politics* as "the governing of a political entity…and the control of its internal and external affairs." The two perspectives fit well with big-P politics. The aspect of control is based on the capacity of one political party to govern based on the vote of the public and, as a consequence, be responsible for the internal and external affairs of government. This aspect of governing, while very influential to how higher education accomplishes its goals, is external to higher education. That is higher education must respond to external requirements for its plans, objectives, measures of success, and funding, as determined by the governor and legislature and rely on the support they receive from those parties to deliver programs and services.

The Free Dictionary defines politics as "intrigue or maneuvering within a political unit or a group in order to gain control of power." This definition gives meaning to the efforts of constituencies within higher education to compete for resources held within a community college, university, or system office. *Merriam-Webster* gives even more clarity as it suggests that politics is the "art or science concerned with guiding or influencing governmental policy." It is the internal competition, or small-p politics, found in the interactions among students, faculty, staff, leaders, and others within a system that continuously attempt to influence other constituencies of their value.

In the end, little-p politics of internal constituencies must take its case to the big-P politicians, or external authorities, in an attempt to persuade them of the value of higher education while competing with other state priorities.

Both internal and external constituencies will be subject to "often conflicting interrelationship among people in society" (the

Free Dictionary 2016). Conflicts on policy, planning, and funding are common within and outside of higher education. The conflicts may be historic ideological positions or short-term issues whose resolution has only minor repercussions. A parallel definition is "the political opinions or sympathies of a person" (*Merriam-Webster* 2016). The focus on the individual has meaning both for state-level (external) politicians and their specific priorities and individuals within (internal) constituencies in higher education attempting to influence their leadership. Big-P or external politics and little-p internal politics are very real manifestations of politics occurring within and outside of higher education.

The need for constituencies to gain control even through means that creates conflict, is inherent in both big-P and small-p politics. The connection is even greater when considering that at the state level there are goals for public higher education access, cost, and quality that must be addressed by higher education systems and institutions. Those goals become a part of an institutions planning and as a consequence funding requests to support enrollment estimates, facility requirements, faculty needs, financial aid, etc. In other words, public higher education competes with other state agencies for funding to meet the state approved higher education goals and other statewide goals.

There is a great deal of irony in the state's expectations for a quality higher education and yet they have been unwilling (not unable) to fund their own public higher education's goals. The goals of access and quality have been affected by the continuing decline of state support. Higher education has maintained acceptable academic standards primarily due to the dramatic increases in student tuition. The state, through the governor and legislature, expects public higher education to support state goals with diminishing state resources, increased student funds, and "new resources." The common refrain from the state is that budgets need to be more efficient and that "disruptions" to programs and services must be considered. Over the last two decades, as state funds have declined on the whole, budgets have been stripped of any fat and academic programs eliminated out of necessity and not logic. The annual cry for greater efficiency and creativity are the state's fallback position given that there is no objective information that would justify further reductions.

Embedded within the definitions and the essence of politics big-P or little-p politics is the sense that competition among many must drive to some forms of consensus and compromise. While it is not always the case that there is a compromise, the vestiges of successful and unsuccessful negotiations remain with internal and external constituencies for years. It is important to realize that if you received attention for your programs in one year you may not in the next. It is essential to continue to create mechanisms to influence leaders over years and not simply a single planning and budget cycle. It is critical to have continuity in timing and forums for discussion to present program goals, priorities, and values as changes in leadership positions, internally and externally, occur frequently.

CHAPTER 3

What Are the Constituencies That Influence Public Higher Education?

As WAS DONE with politics in chapter 2, the term *constituency* will be defined to ensure a common understanding of its use. Once defined, there will be an in-depth review of the manifold constituencies that play a major role in influencing the success of public higher education.

Merriam-Webster: Constituency

1. A body of citizens entitled to elect a representative.
2. A group or body that patronizes, supports, or offers representation.
3. The people involved in or served by an organization (as a business or institution).

Source: *Merriam-Webster Online Dictionary*, retrieved November 2016

In chapter 2, we connected the division of internal and external constituencies based on little-p and big-P political interactions.

"A body of citizens entitled to elect a representative" (*Merriam-Webster* 2016) would best define the constituency characterized as the external political body of the governor and legislature. It is the governor and legislature that would make decisions regarding state programs and funding. They would become competitors (and occasionally supporters) with higher education in the implications of decisions affecting universities and community colleges. The competition would be most pronounced when there were disagreements in policy and programs affecting state citizens.

"A group or body that patronizes, supports or offers representation" (*Merriam-Webster* 2016) would fit the committees and organizational structures found in universities and community colleges. That is the many constituencies including students, faculty, staff, and leadership would provide their thoughts and recommendations through various forums and committees as required by the institution and state board. It is through the committees and forums and other gatherings that the internal constituencies would lobby for their priorities and ultimately compete for leadership support.

How can constituents either as individuals or groups be identified? Which constituencies are most influential and why?

The list of constituencies that interact or compete within and outside of higher education is long. The degree of competition varies based on a host of variables including funding, program overlap, state goals, big-P political balance, public expectations, etc.

The constituencies vying for attention include the following: governor, the legislature generally and legislative committees, higher education system leaders, institutional leaders, students, faculty, state agencies (responsible for legal, educational, financial, and facilities oversight), accrediting bodies, federal government, financial aid organizations, and so on.

There are instances where there are common goals and coordination of programs which is relatively straightforward. There are other times when constituent goals are not in sync and even at odds with one another, and finding common ground is very difficult.

We will examine each of the internal and external constituencies in the following chapters. First, it is critical to understand the absolute connection of the key concepts of competition, compromise, and cooperation is completely dependent on how constituencies interact with one another. Each concept exists only where there is more than one constituency seeking to gain some recognition of its value. One can't compete, cooperate, and compromises with oneself; at least two actors are necessary. Obviously, as we broaden out the number of constituencies, we expand the opportunities for competition that can be both positive and negative. We hope for cooperation to keep communications and commonly held principles on a mutually acceptable path. Compromise becomes a necessary end to achieve some movement forward. An increase in negative competition, limited cooperation, and unwillingness to compromise reflects scenarios where all or most parties gain no benefit toward their respective plans and goals.

It is important to understand that in its most basic form politics, big-P and little-p politics, is driven by, for, through, and around constituencies. It is each constituency and their myriad of overlapping interactions that determines how and what decisions are made. That is not to say that there is a neat formula that calculates a decision based on the number and quality of interactions, but rather the extreme difficulty in arriving at solutions based on the variation in constituent goals, size, resources, ownership, power base, etc.

Examples of Constituency Intersection

In chapter 1, there was a scenario that reflected the expectations of varying constituencies in dealing with a set of governor's recommendations. The broad problem of state reduction in resources had implications for each group and in fact defined relationships. The parameters of the scenario were as follows:

- Higher education generally would be reduced by 7% in state funding.
- History of funding reductions magnify current losses of funding.
- The governor would offer flexibility to institutions for measurable outcomes.

- Students were confronted with tuition increases.
- Students sought increased financial aid and no tuition increases.
- Student trust for institutional administration had deteriorated over the years.
- Faculty and staff sought compensation increases over three years.
- The governor recommended a reduction in time to degree from 5.5 years to 4.5 years.
- Legislative leaders did not believe higher education's rationale for more funding.

The intersection of constituencies occurs on many levels and responses to the scenario are as follows:

Board/Chancellor to Institutional Leaders

The board leadership directs the chancellor to develop alternatives addressing the demands of the governor and legislature and outline the implications at the system and institutional levels. The chancellor shares the board guidance with the institutional presidents and gets their feedback on the form and substance of the process, timing, organization, system, and institutional linkages/communications. The chancellor then reports back to the board with the final decisions and provides direction to the universities and community colleges to begin their processes.

The board and chancellor would eventually receive institutional plans and have to determine their strategic position on how best to approach the governor. As suggested in the alternatives in chapter 1, they could have accepted the reduction and programmed the cuts in their future budgets. Or they could have argued for increased funding (to mitigate the 7% cut), identified new fund sources, and streamlined some academic and administrative programs with reallocated funds to priority areas, faculty compensation, and lowering of student tuition.

System Leaders—Institutional leaders

The president and leadership team develop processes to listen to and respond to internal constituent concerns and demands. They lay out the system wide goals and begin their review. The leaders of the institutions create their own plans in the image of the system but with attention to their unique mission requirements. They act as the champion of student, faculty, and institutional needs while having to place limitations on process, funding expectations, promoting new program growth, and even identifying possible areas for reduction.

They react to the chancellor regarding levels of reduction, tuition options, compensation, and other elements of a final request. They also argue with the chancellor and system on the behalf of the internal constituencies.

Students to Leaders

The student leaders lobby for additional resources and greater acknowledgment in the decision-making processes. The primary purpose of the students in this type of planning effort is to create a greater awareness of the effect of tuition increases, need for more financial aid, and lack of representation in decision-making processes. They do not want to support a 2% tuition increase and feel they have been left out in receiving technology and classroom upgrades.

The students meet with institutional leaders in academic, student, financial, housing, and health areas to gain the administrative perspectives on what can be expected in the future. They use the forums and formal meetings to lobby for their needs and attempt to seek some levels of compromise.

Students to Students

The student leaders organize students to carry their messages to internal and external parties. The primary goal is to build a more educated and vocal student body as a means to influence leaders. Student involvement in government can be limited in many institutions, but under circumstances of distress, it is incumbent on student leaders to arouse an interest and involvement in their own well-being. The students in this instance have not trusted the administration for a number of years and are willing to lobby both internally and externally to get some positive attention.

The high potential that they will have to pay increased tuition and gain little financial aid stimulates actions to gain nonfinancial benefits in the areas of technology, time to degree improvement (actually supporting the governor's initiative), and other counseling and healthcare advances.

Students to Governor/Legislature

The student leaders speak to external parties in committee meetings and privately to deliver their message relative to insufficient financial aid and impacts of reduced funding on their costs of attendance. Very often the governor and legislators do not want to appear to be fighting with students to avoid being seen as insensitive to their needs. In this scenario, as students have been hit with rising tuition over a number of years in response to legislative reduction to funding, they have a strong case for a positive reaction.

The students should be working in concert with the system and institutional priorities and goals. If they are working as a team player, then any addback (or lower reduction) in state funds could mean a lower tuition increase.

Faculty to Leaders

The faculty senate leaders offer proposals to the administration in hopes of limiting damaging impacts of reductions while highlighting their below-standard funding relative to peers. The strategic planning efforts of any institution should be assessing all its academic programs to determine what are of highest value and quality in meeting the requirements of the students. Leaders should be focused on retaining the best faculty and compensating them appropriately. Any final plans, regardless if funding increases or decreases, should be placing academic programming as the top priority.

Leaders to Governor

The chancellor and institutional leaders make presentations through board meetings and other public forums responding to the implications of the governor's recommendations, with an emphasis on consequences and alternatives. The governor often appoints the board members and, in many instances, sits on the board as an ex officio member. There are many opportunities to educate the governor and his staff on the downsides of their recommendations and offer alternatives that, while not perfect, better meet the strategies of public higher education. If the 7% can be reduced to 3% with a promise to increase efficiencies, develop measurable outcome measures, and enhance state economic development initiatives, then a compromise is possible, and everyone wins.

Leaders to Legislators

The chancellor and institutional leaders make public presentations through legislative committees and meet with individual members to discuss alternatives to the governor's recommended budget. As the final authority to determine higher education funding and legislate accountability reporting, it is essential that higher education leaders spend time lobbying legislators on the statewide value of higher education and the negative impacts of funding reductions on its citizens.

Intersection of Three or More Constituencies

Beyond the one-on-one intersections are multilevel interactions where faculty, academic and administrative staff, and students can participate in meetings focused on driving to alternative strategies. Institutional leadership may participate in meetings with faculty, staff, and students in outlining the implications of the governor's recommendations and gaining preliminary feedback. Standing and special committees will confer with a range of internal constituents to educate on the issues at hand and receive input.

Perhaps the greatest intersection of internal constituencies is at public board meetings. Board meetings focused on planning, funding, and program priorities typically seek input from students and faculty (as appointed representatives to the board) and other affected units (e.g., facilities, student services, public safety, etc.) when attempting to either gather information or offer recommendations. The constituencies represent board leaders, institutional leaders, faculty, staff, students, subsets of those groups, the public, and often representatives of the governor's office and the legislature. The meetings deal with the most critical issues of higher education and are often barometers of how individual constituencies feel they are being treated on given issues. Constituent leaders will use the opportunities provided by the board to give their perspective on board actions that affect their goals, both positively and negatively.

Constituent Success and Compromise

It is critical in understanding the politics of higher education that internal and external constituencies rise and fall based on their ability to compete with one another. It is the capacity of each constituency to adapt to their environments and be able to cooperate to the extent that compromise is possible. Success in some form can be achieved if longer term views prevail over a sense of loss in the short term. Similarly, if success in one year is realized there is no guarantee it will be realized at that same level in the future. The message to all constituencies is that as you interact with one another consider accepting compromises that move the organization forward even if it is not at the pace you desire. There is always a next year if you measure achievement by the support received for your goals and plans and were able to continue and compete into the future.

CHAPTER 4

The Governor: The Key External Constituent

Governing Role and Responsibilities

THE GOVERNOR IS the chief executive of the state and as such has legal mandates for oversight of all state agencies. The degree of the governor's authority to influence final decisions is different for each state. While all financial, programmatic, and political powers of the office may vary, their value in both a real sense and in the use as a "bully pulpit" cannot be under estimated. The office doesn't often have final say on all issues, but it does shape the outcomes through its interactions with the legislature and the public.

In those instances that the governor represents a different political party than the legislature, there are checks and balances that ensure some equity in treatment on disputed issues. The public will be able to see variances and alternatives play out in a very public debate between the executive and legislative branches. While the governor's recommendations may not be enacted by the legislature, they will become a continuing focus for both practical and political assessment. If legislative initiatives are not successful, then the governor has the opportunity to highlight publicly his concern with the direction and outcomes of legislative decisions that he had opposed. There is fine balance between simply highlighting the negatives of legislative decisions and attempting to work cooperatively to find common ground. The governor should have alternative solutions on how to best to improve conditions for the public.

Interaction with Constituencies: Formal and Informal Nature of Communications

The interaction of the governor with various constituencies is formal and informal. As suggested, the governor must work closely with the legislative leaderships in conveying state priorities, key initiatives, funding requirements, and other expectations for legislative consideration.

Formal Interactions

There are formal avenues through which the governor regularly (in most states) submits information for legislative action. Typically, the governor lays out a strategic plan for the states future which is updated periodically. The plan provides statewide goals, priorities, potential initiatives, timelines for action and some funding requirements. The governor also makes annual or biennial budget requests that provide the primary formal interaction between the governor's office, the legislature, constituencies, and the public. There are legislative committee hearings that consider all ramifications of the request from their perceived value to the public, avenues for implementation, outcomes, cost to state, impact on key constituencies, and implications of funding partially, fully, or not at all. The public hearings give an opportunity for the governor's office, chief proponents, chief opponents, general public, and legislators to speak to the strengths and weaknesses of the priorities, programs, and their costs. While not all hearings are open to the public, there is generally an opportunity for input prior to action being taken on a legislative bill or funding request.

Public hearings should be held for all state agencies program and funding requests. State agencies like higher education and their university or college units should develop their final requests through a process of internal debate and public scrutiny. In the case of higher education, statewide governing or policy boards often represent the resource that listens to questions actively and acts on constituent expectations and requests. It is the public, formal dialogue in the board meetings that the governor's office can review along with all submitted material in building the statewide budget for legislative review.

Informal Interactions

The governor meets with most constituencies throughout the year. The meetings would be during periods that might have some significance to the governor or constituency. It may be during the budget development process when a state agency is seeking to "sell" its request and get gubernatorial support. Students may seek an audience with the governor after the budget request has been made to highlight the necessity of his backing for state funds to avoid major increases in student tuition and fees. Higher education leaders may seek meetings during the year to discuss their ideas on the future of higher education and to get a sense of what the governor is considering. The hope for both sides would be to find common ground and build program requests that reflected those common goals. Consensus built out of compromise can be a key trait of a successful governor seeking to maximize support cutting across multiple constituencies. While it is not possible to make everyone happy all the time, taking positions that have positive effects for many will benefit most.

The governor will meet with leaders in settings that provide for more private conversations outside the normal committee hearing settings. The meetings can be used to discuss general directions, goals, priorities, and potential solutions but can't enter into any negotiations or final decisions in the absence of a public scrutiny. While it is likely that more informal agreements are reached, in such gatherings ultimately the appropriate public hearings must be held to listen and debate all final positions.

As an example, higher education leaders from the system or universities may set fact finding meetings that are not formally noticed to discuss a range of issues. The intention of the sessions is to lay out ideas and gather information for planning purposes. The governor may offer statewide priorities that higher education leaders can consider as they build their own plans. There may be tentative funding guidelines that give directions for system leaders to debate as funding parameters when working through budget development exercises. The governor may meet with legislative leaders to speak to specific issues of concern and create a dialogue that helps gain a better understanding with all involved in the discussion.

The formal and informal opportunities to create a dialogue with constituencies is the primary way for a governor to communicate ideas, thoughts, mandates, etc., and in turn learn what the constituencies are thinking on key issues. It is the ongoing sharing of information that can provide a basis for consensus building when the time comes to make final decisions.

Applying the SDMM to Inform Higher Education Leaders

The model has six primary components including strategic thinking, information analysis and reporting, future scanning, strategic planning, transparency, and a planning and assessment framework. There are a number of ways in which aspects of the model can be applied to help in making more successful decisions.

While all components should be used on a continuing basis it is possible to use the planning and assessment framework (P and A framework) to provide a focus on specific topics. That is, lay out the six key questions of the framework and drive to conclusions based on a comprehensive assessment of all information available. The key questions drive a subset of issues that demand further exploration. The following expands on the framework provided in the first chapter as additional background when considering the conditions of specific scenarios.

Planning and Assessment Framework (Questions Driving Assessment)

1. What is the problem? What creates instability? Is there agreement on the problem?

   How was the problem identified and by whom? Are all constituencies equally invested in the problem? What data supports that there is a problem? What is the connection with organizational priorities? Are there interactions that should be considered?

2. What examples contribute to the problem? What is the magnitude of the problem?

   There are potentially a number of issues spawned by one or more problems as identified in question 1. What are they, and what is the severity relative to each constituency and decisions makers?

3. What is the origin of the current examples of the problem? What caused the problem?

   Is there a specific instance or point in time that the problem was identified? Is there agreement among constituencies on the timing and cause?

4. Is there a historical precedent for the problem? Does the precedent connect with current issues?

   Do the historical examples provide context that can be tied to current examples? Do the examples provide leadership lessons that can be applied to current circumstances?

5. What constituencies are most affected? Do all constituencies feel there is a problem? What is the relative stake for each?

What is the relative stake or position of each constituency in the problem? If all constituencies don't feel there is a problem, then what is their position on the problem? How do all constituencies feed into the leadership decision-making? What data supports the various positions?

6. Provide alternatives or actions on how to strategically prepare for and address similar examples in the future.

Do conclusions lend themselves to one or more actions? What is the timeline for an action plan? What successful outcomes can be drawn from national examples? What are the metrics that can be used to measure progress on the actions are implemented?

The P and A framework is an integral inventory of questions that should drive planners and leaders to pursue all possible aspects of the problems they face. The following scenario or set of issues and related problems/challenges will be reviewed through the P and A framework. The outcome of the review will be one or more alternatives for leaders to consider along with other sources of strategic information.

Using the SDMM: Application of the Planning and Assessment Framework

Scenario

The governor of State X has decided to reduce state funding for public higher education. The reduction is based on a weak economy, pledge not to raise taxes, priority funding for corrections and health care, and a sense that public higher education can identify replacement revenues to offset state-funding losses. The system / board of higher education has been requested to provide the executive budget office a detailed plan of how the reductions at 10% level would be made (e.g., to which programs, reasons for the choices, potential outcomes, and attention to state priorities).

Higher education leaders then took the broadly conceived mandate and created specific areas for decision-making (the example is intended to be limited and not capture all potential issues):

1. Impacts on enrollments and access to public universities and community colleges
2. Historical loss of funds in prior five years—implications of losses already incurred
3. Implications for academic and administrative programs—which programs would be reduced or eliminated and why
4. Implications for addressing statewide priorities (e.g., maximizing access of state residents, increasing research and its value to the economy, and growing employment opportunities for students within the state)
5. Loss of staff and faculty—implications for local and state economy
6. Resources to offset state-funding losses—primarily additional tuition from resident and nonresident students (What are the implications for access of continuing and new students?)

As we look at the outline developed by leaders of how to respond to the governor's mandate we can connect the assessment framework with specific attention to politics inherent in constituency competition for scarce resources.

Connecting Decisions with Constituency Demand

In this instance we are assessing how the expectations of the governor will be received by the public and how the higher education leaders will consider the expectations of not only the governor but also the students, faculty, the public, institutional leadership, the legislature, and a host of others when planning their responses. The fact that the primary scenario focuses on program reductions automatically creates a tension among constituencies. Who will be reduced the least and the most? How will program reductions be determined? Will be there be a public debate on any plans both at the institution and system levels? Will there any push back on the governor's request? Could/should constituencies lobby the governor for specific initiatives? What are the ramifications for students and access with increasing tuition costs? And more.

The Planning and Assessment Framework

1. What is the problem? What creates instability? Is there
   agreement on the problem?

The funding reduction is the primary problem which drives many subsidiary problems. Which programs will be reduced? how will students be affected financially through added costs while realizing fewer educational options? What are the implications for strategic directions over the next five to ten years and not just the upcoming biennium? Are other sources of revenue available? Can state priorities be realistically supported given the projected reductions?

There is considerable instability for all constituencies given the historical loss of funds and uncertainty in what programs will be cut and by how much. All constituencies agree there is a problem with immense ramifications for all.

2. What examples contribute to the problem? What is the
   magnitude of the problem?

At the state or macro level, the governor supports reduced funding for various agencies and limiting tax growth. It is through this strategy that the governor can force a reallocation of funds to executive priorities while avoiding an increase in taxes. The legislature seeks to decrease the size of state government and will back a reduced funding approach. The legislature has its pet programs as well and the areas of difference with the governor will revolve around more marginal program promises and generally less significant ideological divides.

Often the directions of external leadership are driven by political commitments to avoid any new or expanded taxes given the perceived or real risk of not being reelected. In the era of small government and low taxes higher education is forced more and more to disengage from state funds and assume a status of only limited state support. While every dollar from the state is essential, the losses over the last ten to fifteen years have shifted the balance away from a public higher education funded primarily from state funds to, in some instances to below 25% of the combined state and student tuition budget.

At the institutional level a reduction of 10% requires a complete reassessment of academic and administrative programming, enrollment estimates, and funding implications. It is likely that without some new funding source that layoffs and program eliminations will be required. The magnitude or severity is at its highest level.

3. What is the origin of the current examples of the problem? What caused the problem?

The governor and legislature are committed to not raising taxes and as such as various program demands grow based on legal mandates or choice (e.g., K-12, corrections, public safety, etc.). As might be expected the remaining funds can't sustain existing programs at continuing levels. Thus, the origins are directly linked to political calculations that limit state government and support promises made to the electorate. The origin of political decision-making goes back to the beginning of the republic. The desire to limit state government has been an ideological position of debate for decades.

As can be seen, there is a common theme in many states where the majority of the voting public will support lower individual tax burdens. They will expect the users of specific services pay for those services and in turn will reduce government subsidies. The historical practice of using tax dollars to more fully support state priorities, like public higher education, has shifted to individual users (students) paying higher tuition and various fees. One could identify many services once supported by the state in a more robust manner that have been eliminated or are only partially funded through state tax dollars.

In this scenario, the system of higher education and institutions are asked to continually readapt to diminished state commitment while students assume a greater share of the cost.

4. Is there a historical precedent for the problem? Does the precedent connect with current issues?

There have been many years that states have realized the loss of revenues. The initial years of the great recession beginning in 2008 were due to unanticipated losses in sales and income taxes and related losses in jobs and income. Other years the legislature approved tax reductions which in turn reduced available revenues. While no one would have purposely supported a recession, there are those that sought more limited government and benefited in the long run from the state-funding losses and state-level decisions not to return to funding levels prior to the recession.

The lesson learned for leaders is to be prepared strategically with alternatives that can address differing levels of funding reductions. If there is reluctance on the part of the governor and legislature to fund higher education at current levels, then create options that match potential reductions. Always be ready to fight for programs and funding that is considered critical to the state but have plans that assume they won't be funded.

5. Which constituencies are most affected? Do all constituencies feel there is a problem? What is the relative stake for each?

Almost all state agencies have been affected by the decline in state funding. Public higher education has been viewed by most as discretionary and as such has sustained among the greatest cuts over time in most states. It has been assumed that universities and community colleges could raise tuition and fees and gain from other sources to offset state losses. Unfortunately, while tuition and fees have been raised, they do not offset state losses while putting the onus on the student to take on more debt.

All constituencies agree with the problems and feel threatened by cuts to their programs. The students have the most at stake and are the most obvious losers in this scenario. They have shouldered dramatically increased tuition and fees while not getting corresponding growth for instructional, facility, and auxiliary services. Faculty members have seen their ranks diminished to teach fewer programs while often counseling a greater number of students. They have not received the compensation increases as measured by peers. In many instances, they have had to take on greater teaching workloads for limited or no new pay increases. System and institutional leaders have sought to find an equitable balance in funding for programs and services for each institution and attempted to maintain access for all resident students. They have sought to not price students out of attendance through financial aid offerings and other incentives. They have also advocated for the recognition of the value of a public higher education to the governor and legislature with the arguments often falling on deaf ears. All constituencies agree that there is a problem in funding that drives all other issues.

6. Provide alternatives or actions on how to strategically prepare for and address similar examples in the future.

In this example, alternatives should reflect very comprehensive responses to the governor's basis for reducing public higher education and connecting the implications for each constituency. The responses should find a balance of both objective and subjective information. The greater the amount of objective input, the less leeway for detractors to question the conclusions. The greater the amount of subjective input from constituencies, the greater the leeway necessary to acknowledge the value of people's thoughts and wishes. Any alternative should maximize the objective and subjective implications of action or inaction.

Developing alternative solutions from the standpoint of system-level leaders should include a clear understanding of what best serves public higher education and ideally the state. What are the goals and priorities of public higher education as stated in strategic level plans and approved by leadership? What is needed programmatically and financially to address the priorities? What actions are needed to implement the plans at the system level and institutional level? What will constitute success if programs are implemented, and what will be lost or at least unrealized if they are not initiated? Will success or failure have specific measurable outcomes that can be regarded generally by all to be the primary indicators of achievement?

In advance of developing alternatives, let's summarize the conditions confronted by public higher education as posed by the governor. Below are the assumptions:

- Higher education is asked to create a reduction plan for the governor representing 10% of the state funding.
- The plan should reflect impacts on student enrollments.
- The plan should reflect impacts (losses) on faculty and staff and their value in the local and state economy.
- The plan should reflect how higher education would continue to support state goals.
- The plan should identify new funding sources to help offset losses.

Alternatives

Alternative 1: One alternative responding to the governor's expectations is to offer a funding request that reduces state funding as recommended by the governor. It would also include very limited tuition increases for students and no compensation increases for faculty. The goal of the alternative would be to reflect to the state that the extent to which cuts have been sustained over the years has reached a point where there are no viable mechanisms to offset lost support with new revenues. It would be clear that higher education leaders must have solid documentation both historically and going into the future to support the conclusion that all revenue sources, continuing and new, can't offset declining state funds. It is a high-risk option.

The impacts and action plan would reflect deep cuts in academic and administrative programming, losses of continuing faculty and staff (not just vacant positions), reduced classroom opportunities for students, and ultimately a reduction in students served. The students would realize a limited tuition increase but also have fewer classes to complete their degree programs in a timely manner. The action plan would reflect what programs would be cut, the specific faculty and staff terminated, the number of students lost or not admitted (i.e., impact on meeting demand), the inability to meet state targets of employment demands, and reduced capacity to meet state economic development priorities.

Needless to say, alternative 1 assumes risk in not appearing to provide an assumed amount of new revenues to offset the reductions. The governor and legislature often make cuts because there is a corresponding identification of resources to keep programs moving forward. As stated in this option higher education leaders are saying that state cuts have been of such a magnitude over many years that it would be unwise to tax the primary user the student and lose even more revenue as they either aren't able to attend or find other less costly options. It is an alternative that would create a number of confrontational points both publicly and privately that could force state leaders to approach higher education with some modified proposals. It could also give the state a bully pulpit to attempt to discredit public higher education and turn a high-risk response into even greater losses down the road. Under any circumstance, it would raise the issues to the highest public awareness and become an open conflict between higher education and external authorities

Alternative 2: A second approach would be to accept the loss of state funds but with conditions. If the state realizes greater growth in statewide revenues, then higher education would be given some allocation based on negotiated goals and metrics. If public higher education reached the targeted growth in key state indicators, then there would be financial incentives. That is, if public higher education met or exceeded metrics of growth in bachelor's degrees awarded, or time of completion of a four-year degree, or specific metrics in the type of degrees awarded supporting state employment goals, or other negotiated goals, then they would receive incentive funding for their efforts.

The institutions would also raise tuition and fees or identify other resources to close the gap of funding lost by cuts. The increases would not provide a direct benefit to students or faculty given they are backfilling lost funds for continuing programs. The governor and legislature would appear less insensitive to the needs of public higher education if there wasn't a focus on terminations, restrictions in enrollments, lost economic development opportunities, and the general warfare that accompanies loss without any solutions or recourse. The downside for the governor and legislature is that they would have to agree to provide incentive funding for goal attainment which would put added demands on scarce state revenues and acknowledge that specific goals are of high importance to the state. The support for incentive funding may establish a precedent that public higher education and other state agencies will build into future funding negotiations.

Alternative 3: The third scenario is less likely than the first two but is possible given years of prolonged financial neglect while continuing to provide access to state residents. Public higher education leaders in conjunction with their local legislative leadership could make a full assault on the legitimacy of further funding reductions. They could graphically delineate the impacts of reductions over time in terms of quantity, quality, cost, and lost opportunities. They could speak to the loss of students with further tuition and fee increases and loss of faculty due to a lack of compensation increases. The continuing degradation of public higher education could only equate to the loss of public education as a state resource. State residents would not have the input on program availability, quality, cost, and accountability that exists in a public system if the options were only private and for profit institutions.

The approach would have to be built around a set of reasonable goals and metrics that all constituencies aggressively supported within their communities and throughout the state. Lobbying would be a full-time job for all constituencies through a coordinated focus established by system and institutional leaders. Ultimately, this very high-risk strategy will be successful if all constituencies are on the same page and the state leaders feel that further reductions will hurt state residents or they individually will be less politically viable in the future.

Choosing the Correct Alternative

The use of the SDMM/P and A framework is essential in determining which alternative would be best for the circumstances and environment underlying the state and the public higher education system. The governor, the legislature, public higher education, and all the constituencies it represents have differing perspectives on the relative value of their goals, priorities, and funding needs. It is incumbent on higher education leaders to know what the governor expects from higher education and how best to influence those expectations. The model offers a "filter" through which the optimal choices can be made.

This is an ideal example of big-P politics in the guise of the governor's office driving expectations on the internal constituencies and little-p politics of higher education. The findings should include assessments on the implications of the politics for leaders to consider as they make choices. If they choose to fight the state, they should understand and prepare for the repercussions.

CHAPTER 5

The Legislature: The Final Arbiter of Funding

Governing Role and Responsibilities

THE LEGISLATURE IS the most important body in giving life or death to state agency programs, funding, and aspirations. It is the final point of review and approval for agency requests to expand, maintain the status quo or even more critically to downsize based on factors ultimately determined by the legislature. While the governor sets the table relative to agency planning, goals, outcomes, and funding requests, the legislature chooses what it wants based on history, current conditions, future expectations and the political issues of the day or year. Legislative leadership and specific committees (e.g., appropriations, higher education, capital, facilities planning, etc.) work with state agencies and the governor to understand their specific expectations and make decisions based on the collective consensus of legislative leadership. The decisions are generated after multiple committee and legislative hearings, individual member meetings with constituencies, and numerous meetings among legislative leaders with state agencies, the governor's office, the public, and other constituencies.

The quality of decisions made by the legislature is often based on the quality of the information it receives and how it chooses to apply both objective and political standards of the time. It is clear that in many instances in higher education decisions made by the legislature have more to do with the political considerations of the time versus the relative value of the positions laid out by higher education leaders. As an example, there may be bona fide evidence of the value of not reducing funds to avoid loss in student enrollment. Higher education may make the case that a loss of students would generate a loss of students revenues, a loss of graduates available for state jobs, and a loss in local (where colleges and universities reside) economic benefit from student participation (restaurants, retailers, apartments, events, etc.). The choice of the legislature, however, may be to increase reductions with more concern for state-level taxation policies and their electoral status and less about state resident access to higher education programs. It is easier for legislators to defer on discretionary programs such as higher education even though there can be damaging impacts to the state economy and educational readiness.

Interaction Among Key Constituencies

The legislature interacts with all key constituencies of public higher education. It is necessary for every higher education constituency from institutional and system leaders, students, faculty, etc., to have individual meetings or offer public testimony at public committee hearings. Higher education leaders in most states take the recommendations of the governor and seek legislative support for the executive budget in the final appropriations bill. The legislature on the other hand may not agree fully with the governor and offer a reduced set of recommendations.

From the initiation of the governor's budget planning to the development of higher education budget requests to the executive recommended budget and ultimately to the final legislative appropriation there are countless public and private meetings that define all constituent positions. If, for example, the legislature can't support the full funding recommendation of the executive budget, they will seek ways to legitimize a reduced share without taking a position on the value of programs in higher education. To avoid arguments on specific program requests, they may say that safety and correctional programs are more critical to the state or that state tax revenues are more limited than projected in the executive budget.

On the other hand, the various higher education constituencies will provide information that highlights the value of their needs and at times pits internal competitors against one another. As an example, higher education leaders may seek funding for faculty compensation increases, which is fully supported by the faculty. They may also suggest an above average tuition increase for students to offset a portion of lost state funding, which the students would argue against in any forum available. Differences between internal constituencies should be resolved prior to any major public presentations resolved. Leaders should be identifying ways to gain cooperation and compromise to create as much goodwill as possible.

Higher education leaders should, under any circumstance, offer viable counterarguments to legislative positions that are inaccurate or not fully acknowledging higher education value, cost, quality, and general worth to the public. Public advocacy for higher education priorities will stimulate support from faculty, staff, students, and even the public.

The legislature must take all agency inputs and balance their recommendations against financial (i.e., real and perceived) capacity and ideological expectations. The trick for all higher education constituencies is finding the appropriate messaging to fit seamlessly with higher education leadership priorities and be as coordinated in their responsiveness as possible. A collective and positive response among constituencies goes much farther than splinter groups attempting to work only for their individual causes. "United we stand and divided we fall" is all too real when competing for scarce resources in the state government environment.

As is the case with all constituencies, the legislature, more than any other, relies on compromise to get business done. They may make promises in public forums or in private settings to other legislators, the governor's office, and other public interest groups. While government appears to move slowly or with much purpose at times, it will always be seeking to find some improvements no matter how minor for all or most constituencies. If in the end consensus can't be reached on a given issue and parties are unwilling to compromise, then the outcome is negative for one more constituency. Depending on the constituency passion for a topic that has not been adequately supported the legislative representatives will be subject to consistent lobbying and potentially a short career if not capable of finding some solution.

Applying the Planning and Assessment Framework

Scenario

The legislature is considering tax cuts that will reduce state appropriations by some 10% (4% beyond the governor). A 10% reduction in state taxes will likely drive an even greater percent reduction for higher education. They will consider any program expansions or redirections of funding that will create jobs and enhance economic development opportunities. They demand greater efficiency from all state agencies in the use of funds and expect new sources of funding to help offset state cuts. They reflect little interest in listening to higher education concerns for a decrease in enrollments and reduced access for state residents when funds are reduced. (The governor has supported specific enrollment targets by the system and offers incentives for maintaining and growing enrollment levels.)

The system and institutions are required to create a single-formula-based funding model to use for future budget requests. (The legislature is looking for a funding mechanism that is built through the use of more objective information tied to statewide priorities.) The governor will support formula budgeting following an appropriate study done under the guidance and oversight of the executive budget planning and budget office.

Higher Educations Reactions

The system and institutional leadership move first to develop a unified approach to responding to the legislative call for cutbacks. They seek support from the governor in areas where there are differences with the legislative goals. The governor supports those higher education initiatives in executive budget that are being denied by the legislature, but nothing beyond those recommendations. The governor is not interested in going forward with requests that will appear expensive or go in opposition to what was recommended in the past.

Students are asked to be fully engaged with legislators in their local home districts. They are asked to lobby for more moderate state-funding reductions with the carrot of the system will limit tuition increases. Faculty are expected to be fully behind proposals that do no or at least less damage to their own instructional and academic support programs. Compensation add-ons are not promised. The public is asked to speak to legislators that are on the fence about reductions with attention given to their electability in the future. System and institutional leaders lead efforts to provide the implications of any cuts on the state and local districts supporting a university or community college. Estimates of jobs lost, local economy losses in revenues, and any objective evidence that highlights negative impacts on people and programs help bolster the value of higher education programs. Higher education leaders are assuming significant academic and administrative program reductions that will dictate a realignment of resources across the system.

Planning and Assessment Framework

1. What is the problem? What creates instability? Is there agreement on the problem?

The overriding problem is the legislative decision to reduce funding for all state agencies. The perception by leading politicians is that state government is too big and by association higher education is too big and overfunded. The problem is compounded by executive branch and higher education disagreement with legislative premises.

There is substantial instability among all constituencies given the high probability of funding reductions and how they will be allocated. The intention of the legislature to redefine funding approaches through the use of a formula is seen as a means of further reducing the state commitment to higher education.

The specter of the devastating effects of the reductions has brought all internal constituencies together. While each constituency feels they are most damaged they all agree on the problem.

2. What examples contribute to the problem? What is the magnitude of the problem?

The intent to reduce statewide taxes and to allow funding to drop by at least 10% is the catalyst for a number of program and funding concerns. Beyond the loss of funds in the state appropriation will be a loss of funding from students generated by tuition and fees if enrollments not realized. The loss in students will create reductions of funding from students for use of services such as resident halls, food services, book supplies, and countless other auxiliary services. There is the further potential in the loss of grant funding if the number of faculty are reduced and limited in their capacity to provide research and service.

It is difficult to attach a precise measure of severity to the myriad of problems, but it can be assumed that it would be categorized as very severe when considering options of limited, moderate, and very severe. The combination of state and student funds lost will demand rethinking of academic goals and permanent program reductions.

3. What is the origin of the current examples of the problem? What caused the problem?

Historically, the state has been in downward spiral in state funding for a number of years. Following the great recession in 2008, there was a significant decline in state appropriation for higher education (Selingo 2018). Even prior to the great recession, states were working toward smaller state budgets. The assumption had been that only critical programs would be supported and that some responsibilities could be taken on by local governments. The policies created a growing change in the balance of funding between the state and student in higher education. Needless to say, the student share of funding for higher education grew disproportionately as the state divested its funding (Seltzer 2017).

It is anticipated that as the state continues to withdraw support from higher education the student, through the assumption of greater debt for higher costs will seek alternatives to public higher education. The alternatives will provide greater opportunities for employment and in much shorter time frame. The origins of the problem go back at least two decades but have accelerated since the great recession.

4. Is there a historical precedent for the problem? Does the
    precedent connect with current issues?

The magnitude of reductions over the last decade has exceeded any other periods of time. There have been cycles of reductions and increases for decades based on economic conditions but always followed by some uptick in state funding. There have been no sustained periods of growth and only focused funding on limited projects or programs since prior to 2008, the start of the great recession. There are very few states if any that can say they did not sustain a substantial loss (25-50% and higher) of funding support from the state or that the student population in some instances did not realize substantial (over 100%) increase in tuition in response to the lost state support since 2008 through 2017. (While there may be exceptions to the loss of state funding for the period of 2008-2017, the point of lost state support in conjunction with the student assumption of the greater share of costs can't be disputed.) Nationally, in 2000, the net tuition as a percent of public higher education revenue was 29.3%; in 2008, it was 35.8%; and in 2016, 47.8% (SHEEO 2017). That is a **general** view of the shift in all of 2- and 4-year public higher education institutions in the United States, representing both the decline in state funds and increase in tuition. As might be expected, there are hundreds of examples of institutions that were well above the 50% student share of the cost.

The lesson learned by leaders is to be prepared to respond to uncertainty. Create strategic thinking and planning processes that look at the future with an awareness of political intent currently and into the future. Match program expectations with a realistic assessment of the political environment currently and into the future. As importantly develop a realistic assessment of what constituencies can expect in unstable times characterized by reduced commitment of funding from the state, growing disruptions, and an unsustainable cost structure for students.

5. What constituencies are most affected? Do all constituencies feel there is a problem?

No constituency goes unaffected. One could argue that the students are most affected given the major increases in tuition and fees. That is particularly noteworthy given that they weren't benefitting from any new programs or services. They simply did not have programs and services cut as much as they could have been. Faculty would argue that as their ranks have been depleted by program reductions and received no meaningful compensation increases for years, they would be hit as hard as anyone. As the higher education institutions will no longer grow and have even declined in selected instances in students and staffing, local economies have felt the loss of revenues in retail, events, restaurants, etc. As the number of faculty declines, so may funding driven through grants. The grants provide economic benefit to the state and local communities through the hiring of staff to administer the grant programs. Institutional leaders must consider the implications of reduced funding on all programs and all constituencies and, as a consequence, make the most difficult decisions regarding priorities for the short- and long-term viability each institution.

6. Provide alternatives or actions on how to strategically prepare for and address similar examples in the future.

The higher education system and institutions must be fully prepared with alternative strategic plans to reinvent and adapt to unstable financial conditions. In fact, they must be continuously monitoring the state, national, and international environments with assessments that assume best- and worst-case scenarios and create meaningful alternatives.

As suggested in chapter 4, there can be alternatives that support governor's recommendations or those that more aggressively speak for priorities that go beyond the scope of the executive budget. In this scenario, the legislature is laying out specific and highly intrusive demands that go beyond the governor's recommendations.

In advance of developing alternatives, let's summarize the conditions confronted by public higher education as posed by the governor and legislature. Below are the assumptions:

- The legislature recommends reductions to state funding per the legislature and are likely to exceed 10%.
- Reduced enrollment projections will not be supported.
- A formula funding methodology for future budget requests is required.
- Greater efficiency in the delivery of programs is expected.
- New funding sources should be identified to offset lost state fund.

Alternatives

Alternative 1: Higher education leaders have decided to work as closely with the governor's office as possible in fighting for the executive office recommendations. That is, they will organize students, faculty, local leaders, and others to accept reduced recommendations regarding funding as a less damaging option than that of the legislature. It is assumed that the governor's office will provide its full lobbying efforts on behalf of its own recommendations. The challenge for higher education leaders is keeping all constituencies focused on the same priorities, timeline of key events, constituency benefits, and general sense that, if we don't act in a unified manner, no one will benefit.

The legislative leadership will understand the game and prepare for a wide variety of public and higher education advocates bringing pressure to bear from all policy and personal angles. The objective of the legislative leadership is to avoid offering individual constituencies some relief and weaken the overall message of fiscal restraint and shifting funding to nonstate sources. Setting a precedent with one constituency can "spread" immediately and even into the future as other agencies see the connection to their own programs. Governors and legislatures will react negatively to most initiatives that may create program and financial expectations into the future.

Alternative 2: Higher education leaders assume the strategy of moving back to their original request as presented to the governor and consequently reduced in the governor's recommendations. The strategy assumes minimally the governor will support anything connected to executive recommendations. The intent of higher education is to reflect a more complete picture of their needs that were not fully portrayed in the governor's budget. They don't want to argue with the governor but rather get support for not publicly opposing the higher education strategy. There is fine balance between what the governor may or may not back beyond executive recommendations, but if the legislature is signaling major reductions beyond the governor's budget, then some common ground may be found. There may be a sense that the legislature is being punitive and targeting higher education unfairly, which will pull the governor and higher education into at least a temporary alliance.

Leaders create presentations for public discussion on the value of supporting the governor's recommendations while highlighting the benefits of the added increment they requested in the original budget. The discussion will focus on the damage done by the legislative reductions while offering options on how to limit that damage.

Alternative 3: Higher education leaders take the riskier stance that they will fight aggressively for the full request they made to the governor (which is greater than what the governor recommended) and will not deviate from that regardless of the governor's office support. The difference between 2 and 3 is the willingness to create an even more aggressive communications campaign that will likely limit the positive participation or coordination with the governor. Higher education will not discredit the governor's recommendations but will largely ignore them where they differ. The obvious downside is the probability that the governor will lobby against higher education if there is any acrimony. If the uneasiness grows, then future relations with the governor's office could be damaged and the strategy may be unsuccessful in the long run even if there is some short-term gain.

As highlighted in the discussion of questions 1 and 2 in the P and A framework, the magnitude of reductions creates instability across the system that is very severe. In alternative 3, it is assumed that the uncertainty and instability created can't be any greater if the system takes a very active public stance against the legislature. All the objective tools along with the stories of state citizens giving their personal account of the value of higher education will be critical. Being transparent with internal constituencies about the response to the governor and legislature and maximizing the lobbying efforts will be important when taking a more aggressive approach.

Connecting Alternatives with the SDMM

Higher education leaders will be applying the SDMM in constructing and in implementing any of the alternatives. Regardless of how great the risk might be, the model components will function to strategically process information and contribute to possible alternatives. In alternative 3, the model can identify and assess background information on the governor and executive office's reactions to apparent differences in strategy and action. The assessment of the governor's reactions can be balanced against both the short- and long-term implications of the legislative reductions and the governor's support into the future.

It should also be recognized that the SDMM is not the final decision maker but rather a tool to inform leaders. If leaders feel that some hybrid of the three alternatives is necessary, then they are still informed decisions that considered all relevant factors assessed through the model.

Each of the three alternatives has its own value and is responsive to the environment that higher education is assessing. The choice of alternative will vary based on leadership perspectives, historical and potential future conditions, gubernatorial and legislative actions, and a host of variables that are highlighted and filtered through the SDMM. In the end, the decisions belong to leaders within the confines of the all sources of information they review, assess, and incorporate into their planning and thinking.

CHAPTER 6

System and Governing Board Oversight

Governing Board's Roles and Responsibilities

STATE BOARDS OF higher education (in various sizes, structures, and authority) exist primarily to provide assurances to the governor and the public that there are structures in place to ensure that the quality and availability of academic and administrative programs and services are a high priority. There are many single or multiple university/community college boards that are not part of a larger statewide system but must comply with the same planning, program, and funding requests. There are single institutions that have local boards and respond directly to the state regarding any funding and policy requests. There are boards that have governing power, which is greater than those that have coordinating authority. The degree of authority is based on authority granted through the law.

We will focus on multiple institutional systems that report to a board but with the understanding that all public institutions will benefit from the discussion on politics, constituencies, and the application of the SDMM. All public institutions have internal and external constituencies and must make decisions directly related to legislative and executive mandates, planning and budget requirements, policy issues, and other areas of intersection with statewide goals.

The big-P and little-p politics are in play for all institutions regardless of governing oversight.

In most cases statewide goals and plans are an important responsibility focused on what is best to meet the needs of state residents. Often the boards are comprised of members either chosen by the governor or in some combination with the legislature. (Although there are some boards that are elected as in the case of Nevada.) Regardless of the appointing authority boards are accountable through their actions on planning, funding guidelines and budget development, capital construction, academic program standards, quality assessments, and countless other mechanisms of oversight that are both objective and subjective. They represent the board directly or through designated leaders the system and institutions of public higher education at legislative hearings, statewide committee meetings, governor's meetings, board meetings, and other forums that require a state-level perspective on public higher education.

Boards provide the leadership that helps guide each of the community colleges and universities. A primary function is to work closely, through their administrative leadership such as a system chancellor (in some places a president or executive director), with the institutional presidents. The board gives general direction through state-level goals, objectives, accountability measures, strategic plans, academic and administrative programming guidelines, etc., and offer the flexibility to institutional leaders to create their strategic plans that connect with state-level expectations.

System administrations often act as points of translation between boards and institutional leaders in the interpretation of expectations of how best to achieve board goals. A system chancellor must also be prepared to discuss with the board how the individual units are unique in their goals and plans such that the uniqueness is not lost. Too frequently boards work so hard to achieve general statewide goals, plans, and metrics they lose sight of what individual units offer that may fall outside of typical system-level priorities and accountability measures.

System Chancellor's or President's Roles and Responsibilities

A System chancellor or president acts as the key connection with individual board members, the full board when making collective decisions, individual presidents (university or community college) and unit leaders when they gather as a body. The role of issue development, communication, debate, and decision-making among the various groups is complex and often difficult to come to a consensus. The added pressure of being the primary focus to respond to questions from the public, students, faculty, and others on behalf of the system raises the stakes to the highest level. There must be confidence that priorities, outcomes, and allocations are based on strategic thought and planning, transparent processes, coherent policies, and forums for constituent input and debate.

The system chancellor must act as mentioned earlier as the translator of what is or might be with the board to ensure they are educated on the current issues and capable of responding as needed. The chancellor must be able to lay out the board's directions to the institutional leaders so that they can incorporate those directions into their own university or community college planning. The system chancellor must be able to relate the issues of the institutional leaders to the board as a means to ensure there are active two-way communications. It is important that there is as complete an understanding of any concerns or differences of opinions on the implications of the system plans for each institution. One objective of the system and institutional leaders is to reach a consensus on the key positions of the board from which all institutions will build their own programs.

It is also important to acknowledge the more unique programs or populations a given university or community college might serve based on mission, size, location, etc. While the goals and outcomes of the board and its units are generally in sync, there are always some issues that affect a smaller university, or a rural community college, or a land grant university, or a large urban university in ways that can't be assumed into a one size fits all plan or funding request. One of the most difficult activities of any board is finding a balance between what is necessary to meet statewide educational goals and how each institution can best contribute to each goal. Goals of maximizing enrollments may not be a priority for rural institutions trying to meet the needs of fewer students spread over a larger area. A community college mission is not centered on a research focused agenda. An urban university, unlike a community college, is not focused on providing a technical education for those seeking employment in other than four-year-degree programs. Thus, system and institutional leaders must actively engage in dialogue on what the overall statewide goals are but with an awareness that different institutions participate in achieving those goals in a way that best serves their mission and students. Thoughtful dialogue in communication with all constituencies should lead to cooperation and compromise on reaching statewide and system targets.

Interaction with Key Constituencies

As can be assumed, the system chancellor may have more constituencies to respond to than any actor in public higher education. There is the continuing interaction with the **board** as the primary governing body related to the mission and goals of statewide higher education decision-making. It is the board that sets policy, financial expectations, funding requests of the governor, program quality standards, accountability measures, and much more in providing oversight of higher education. The chancellor is the board's key contact in both receiving feedback and direction from the board but also providing feedback and direction from institutions, governor's office, legislators, and many others to the board.

A close second as a constituency of greatest interaction are the **institutional presidents**. They rely on system direction regarding finances, academic programs, administrative programs, strategic plans, marketing, lobbying, and most everything with a state-level implication. There is ongoing dialogue within the system administration with not only the institutional leaders but the staffs in finance, academic administration, facilities, etc. The vice presidents from the chancellor's staff work closely with their counterparts in each university and community college to flesh out the details of key issues and initiatives.

The system through the chancellor meets with **students** periodically to discuss issues of greatest concern to the students such as costs, availability of courses, residence halls, financial aid, safety, and much more. There is an expectation on the part of the students that the chancellor will represent their views to the board in a fair manner. The chancellor in turn must recognize the students as the primary reason the institution exist and make all efforts to develop balanced and necessary policies.

The **faculty** will have meetings through their faculty senate and key committees to create requests to share with their institutions, system, and the board. Discussions will often focus on compensation, program growth or decline, research productivity, enrollment opportunities, and matters of efficiency and effectiveness. They frequently seek a greater role through faculty governance in the decision-making of the system and institution on issues as they evolve.

Another key constituent that offers the most external direction to the board is **the governor** of the state. The governor in many states appoints all or some of the board members to extended terms. Thus, the governor identifies members that will likely reflect executive views. The board presents an annual or biennial request to the governor for consideration and recommendation. The governor sets guidelines of how and when the request is to be submitted. As importantly in many states, the executive office requires comprehensive multiyear strategic plans of all state agencies. The plan provides the means through which higher education gives a long-term perspective on goals, priorities, measures of accountability, and initiatives that give explicit support to state goals. The plan also offers the governor an opportunity to take positions that may or may not be supportive of the ultimate measures and outcomes forwarded by the board and individual institutions. As might be expected, there will be differences between the governor and higher education in the level of support for plans based on the goals of specific programs, on the time to accomplish certain goals and the amount of funds needed to achieve those accomplishments.

The chancellor works as the chief connection to the governor's office in ensuring that the board and institutions are represented in not only receiving executive direction but also offering input that could influence process, timing, priorities, etc., of the executive budget. In some states leaders of the higher education system sit as a member of the governor's cabinet and as such the development of plans, budget requests, and policy initiatives may more closely mirror the governor's own agenda.

The chancellor works closely with **legislative leadership** in routinely responding to current requests and in lobbying for key higher education initiatives. The chancellor is the face of public higher education for its governing board but works closely with institutional presidents in forwarding their issues and requests.

The chancellor is the source for information going out of the system and often the first point for receiving information coming into the system. Thus, the role of maintaining communications with **the public** during periods of quiet and stress is paramount. When the system requests funding from the governor, it becomes a major story that must have updated and accurate data and information moving into the public domain.

Although mentioned briefly, the chancellor role with university leaders is as important, complex, and demanding a task as any. Each community college or university in the system must be receiving guidance from the system on an ongoing basis, and in turn the system office must be getting feedback from the institutions on an ongoing basis. The greatest opportunities for error come when the system or institutions do not fully inform one another on current activities, legislative discussions, major events, marketing efforts, or anything else that may become a public concern. If the chancellor is to adequately represent the board and institutional leaders, there must be continuing conversations that avoid unnecessary public debate on issues that could have been resolved or at least anticipated if communicated in a timely and thoughtful manner.

The **chancellor has a staff** that represents areas or divisions such as finance, academic affairs, governmental relations, planning, legal affairs, etc., that connect the system to the corresponding staffs of institutions and to the public. The chancellor relies on staff to communicate and converse with their counterparts in a comprehensive manner to ensure everyone is informed on the wishes of the board and in turn informed on the thoughts and actions of each institution. Continuing communication between the chancellor's office, the public, and institutions is as important an objective as any other of the chancellor's office. If communication is faulty, then timing, process, public perceptions, outcomes, and more will be cast in doubt. Trust will be lost.

The chancellor will often meet with subsets of the higher education constituencies beyond general board meetings. There may be meetings with **student leadership** to talk about board policies, faculty **leaders** seeking a greater voice in their program funding, **lobbyists** representing each university during legislative sessions, **research advocates** seeking greater matching funding, and many other interactions focused on various advocacy groups representing various constituencies.

There must be continuing communications with all constituencies from the system/chancellor to the institutions, faculty, staff, students, governor's office, and the public, regarding current issues, actions, and forums on the key issues of the times. The success of any chancellor will be based on the timeliness, quality, and accuracy of communications coming from the chancellor's office. While there are many other indicators of success, communication of key positions on a timely basis regarding current hot ticket items that have immediate implications for constituencies is essential. (It should be remembered that if the conditions of communications timeliness, quality, and accuracy are successfully achieved, then the staff and chancellor are doing their jobs.)

Not surprisingly the chancellor's job is to maximize the information going to all constituencies and always seek some level of consensus. Gaining consensus is often not possible and requires compromise. The compromise can take the form of a promise to one or more constituencies that they will receive consideration for their priorities in the future in lieu of immediate action. It may take the form of shifting funding from one program to another with the support for funding in another program. Compromise is tricky and can lead to situations that don't gain consensus and become a point of contention in future negotiations.

Using the SDMM: Applying the Planning and Assessment Framework

Scenario

The governor has determined that public higher education must be more accountable for the funding it receives from the state. Accountability in the form of indicators of performance and related reports on how the funds are spent is required. While the system will have some flexibility, the governor expects measures that span funding, facilities, enrollments, quality, etc. There should be an analysis of all fund sources beyond state dollars that ensures a complete overview of what programs are supported by what fund sources.

The board may offer the report in a format of its choice, but it should be provided in advance of the executive budget and incorporate a cross-section of planning and accountability measures for discussion with the governor and legislature. It is assumed that the report will be shared with all interested parties throughout the state and become an important reference for discussions in the future.

Higher Education Response

The chancellor shares the governor's request with the board and opens a discussion on how best to proceed. Following the meeting the chancellor lays out potential scenarios for how to react and move forward with the institutions including a timeline of activity. The board in turn provides the chancellor with the general approval conditioned on continuing feedback and progress in meeting the governor's expectations.

The chancellor then meets with the institutional presidents to discuss a comprehensive approach to accountability. The presidents offer their concerns, particularly with providing information that may be preliminary in nature and without adequate vetting and discussion. They also agree on supporting the development of reports that can not only be presented to the governor but will also supplement the decision-making processes of the system and board. There is a sense that there will have to be an ongoing quality assessment of the data and analysis for the new reports, but that the benefit of the reports is greater than the risk of its use.

The chancellor develops a comprehensive plan for the board review and approval and the units begin recasting their data and information systems to capture and assess the new information. The processes demand extreme amounts of time and effort on the part of the system and units in gaining consensus on new accountability definitions and measures, building data and analysis infrastructure, and agreeing on methods through which reports are provided uniformly by each unit. Needless to say, not all institutions want to share information they feel will not benefit them, but given the opportunity to fully explain any anomalies, they support the new direction.

When the governor requested both accountability measures and funding connected to those measures it was defining the use of outcome-based funding. Outcome-based funding is a model of funding where a substantial portion of the budget could be connected to measuring performance in achieving state and higher education goals (Hearn 2015). The work for this scenario is first identifying the key outcomes and measures and then creating a translation from outcome to budget allocation. The current form of budgeting in the state is the addition of increments or decrements to an existing base of dollars annually. The two methods are very different and demand much thought, time, communication, and transparency in working with all constituencies.

Planning and Assessment Framework

1. What is the problem? What creates instability? Is there
   agreement on the problem?

The primary conceptual problem is creating new or expanded information resources that will be used to judge quality and success of the system and institutions. The governor and all others will be able to look at qualitative and quantitative indicators and draw conclusions on how public higher education is progressing or if it is progressing. Another problem is that the reported information can be interpreted to reflect success when viewed from one perspective and viewed as a failure when viewed from another perspective. If public higher education suggests that they have been showing continuing improvement in enrollment growth through an annual average of 5%, the governor may suggest that it is not meeting the demands of the state that suggest 7% is what is required.

A secondary problem is the complexity of discussing differences between institutions that differ in size, goals, locations, mission, etc. A large land grant university will have very different measures than a small rural community college. As an example, it is of the utmost importance to build understandings that enrollment growth, the amount and types of students sought, are substantially different between the two types of institutions. A community college is charged to support local or state resident needs in academic, vocational, and service programming. A land grant university will be enrolling students from the state, nationally, and throughout the world. The university will have a primary emphasis on degree granting programs and no focus on vocational education. Thus, the goal of enrollment growth will differ and that the governor, the legislature, and the public must realize and accept that the numbers produced will be connected to very different missions and goals.

Not all constituencies will see the process and even outcomes as a problem. Students may not be connected enough to the implications of such a study and will be less inclined to become involved. Faculty leadership will see the need to stay in touch with any process that suggests new ways of measuring success in teaching, research, and service. Institutional leadership should see the potential problems of creating a new accountability structure that will be used as the tool for determining success by internal and external constituencies.

Instability should be minimal, although once outcome measures are used for measuring success most of the constituencies will become more interested depending on their own specific measures.

2. What examples contribute to the problem? What is the magnitude of the problem?

State-level leadership seeks greater understanding and justification for the funds it provides to all state agencies. Boards of higher education attempt to address the statewide implications of public higher education by supporting the governor's expectations for objective information that can back up higher education requests for funding. As the state and board seek more information to guide their decisions the control of the message, mission, programs, and outcomes by institutions is lessened or at least placed under a statewide perspective for judgment.

The severity or difficulty of creating new accountability systems comes about in the developmental process (e.g., gaining buy-in, transparency, perceived winners and losers, etc.) and then in the assessments of success when implemented. The rubber hits the road when institutions are evaluated based on many performance indicators and must respond to any perceived failures. If the failures translate into fewer dollars for programs, then constituencies will take notice. The magnitude of the overall problem then becomes more apparent.

3. What is the origin of the current examples of the problem? What caused the problem?

The continuing drop in state funding nationally has driven the demands for more information that either supports or denies public higher education's request for new programs and funding. The expectation by state-level leaders for more information regarding enrollments and other key indicators of higher education value is now routinely provided through various planning and budgeting exercises driven through a board. In this scenario, the governor is seeking more information from which decisions can be based on outcomes tied to the goals of higher education and the state. It is simply an evolving environment where less funding drives greater scrutiny.

4. Is there a historical precedent for the problem? Does the
   precedent connect with current issues?

In most states as well as federally there has been a growing
emphasis on the use of more data to justify program existence and
funding. The demands have been most apparent when funding
reductions were being made and leaders required more data to understand the impacts of those reductions. In effect, the loss of funds has
moved boards, governors, and legislatures to more of a microanalysis
of programs and their relative values.

The leadership lesson for higher education is that preparedness
for the future is critical. It is one thing to make a request for your
funding and program and funding needs and another to know how
to react and act when programs and funding are cut. Leaders must
have strategic plans based on thoughtful considerations for all constituencies, but reduction scenarios that equal or exceed what might
be expected.

We are experiencing times that focus on how to adapt to loss
of state funding while relying on other fund sources in continuing
key goals and programs. Again, we are in an ongoing cycle where the
precedent of funding decline that began years ago is now an anticipated process that demands strategic thinking and planning.

5. Which constituencies are most affected? Do all constituencies
   feel there is a problem? What is the relative stake for each?

There are many constituencies affected to varying degrees by
the mandate to establish broader and deeper accountability structures. The chancellor must lead efforts to redefine information development, communicate the enhancements and establish agreed-upon
implementation strategies and timelines. Each institution must follow through on the promise to create its own data and information
system to mirror board/chancellor guidelines. The governor will follow the progress of the new reporting processes and be the first to
assess its value. The legislature will use the information as it benefits
its positions, either pro or con on issues of interest such as fund-

ing, enrollment growth, administrative efficiency, economic development initiatives, and other more local concerns. The public will react to the outcomes of the reports both to individual units and to the progress on key indicators at the state level. Advocates for specific programs will glean the information they want to support their positions. An advocate for student access will applaud exceeding targets in undergraduate growth on the one hand, while advocates for increasing research opportunities will reflect frustration if federal research grants decline.

The reports, while based on objective data, will become political tools that will be useful in some decision-making at the board level but become less acceptable when viewed by the external constituencies of the governor and legislature.

(The Arizona University System/Enterprise developed a performance-based funding model for the three universities and presented it to the governor as an alternative to the historical enrollment-based model [Arizona Board of Regents, FY 2012]. The governor supported a limited request for FY-15 biennium, which was not funded and ultimately the model was never used again as the public vehicle to seek funding [Governor Brewer 2013 and 2014]. It was felt by many that the model raised the expectations for greater funding and provided a means to reflect how underfunded higher education was. The university system moved back to a per-resident-student funding model but did continue to use a variety of accountability measures for internal discussions [Arizona Board of Regents 2015].)

As suggested earlier the missions of the universities and community college are different, and if there is some intent to compare outcomes, then the concept of accountability loses its value.

All constituencies have some stake in the success of the new data and analyses reporting particularly when their programs are measured to determine success. How well their programs and institutions fare under the new measures will determine how much they feel they have a stake in the process and its outcomes.

6. Provide alternatives or actions on how to strategically prepare for
   and address similar examples in the future.

In this particular scenario there will be one alternative that represents a best-case approach to responding to the governor's request for increased accountability. Unlike chapters 4 and 5, there is no alternative that would suggest we will not the governor's request given the opportunity to use the plan to the benefit of higher education.

The chancellor and board support for the governor's request is important in reflecting its value to all constituencies. At the outset, there may be a perceived or real demand for new accountability measures and new information technology resources. However, it is important to make a thorough review of what currently exists and how it can be used more effectively (such a determination should begin with the current reports already being reviewed and how they fit into future planning). Inherent in the request is the opportunity for higher education to reassess existing methods for collecting data and identifying what data is collected and why and how it is used and communicated. The opportunity is to not only meet the governor's expectations but also leverage potential enhancements that would be identified through the process and recommendations.

Process, Choices, and Capacity

System-level committees should work with institutional representatives on both the identification of information needs and data but also the technological wherewithal for units to systematically collect and use the information. There is little doubt that different institutions have different information technology capabilities and different data needs. A community college will not be tracking research related projects and funding like a university. Universities will not be tracking their student enrollments in the same way as community colleges given that the majority of community college students are enrolled in technical and nondegree programs. The continuing challenge is for system leaders with their institutional counterparts to recognize differences and build those into any final considerations.

Different data and information needs establish different data requirements and analyses.

In advance of developing alternatives, we will summarize the conditions confronted by public higher education as posed by the governor.

- The governor is looking for greater accountability for state funding.
- The system and each institution must develop outcome/accountability measures.
- The new accountability measures will be used to assess the performance in the use of state funds.
- The system will have some flexibility in the choice of their accountability reporting.
- Each institution should do a comprehensive analysis of all nonstate funds fund sources and the programs they support.

Alternative

(Only one alternative is developed in recognition that, by not following through with the governor's request, would only damage higher education. There is no viable second alternative.)

The first step is assessing what exists within the current information system reporting processes and what needs to be developed to address the governor's request. If in the process there is information and indicators that aren't needed or new ones to be considered, they should be thoroughly debated at the system and institutional levels. If it is clear there are data points that the governor would like included, then they should be clearly defined and discussed as to value and ease of capturing. There are instances where retrieving quality data is both subjective and limited in its ability to process and maintain.

Second, once there is some agreement on the desired data/information for reporting purposes, then comes the determination of which institutions have the technological capacity to both capture the data and do in-depth analyses. The value of information is downgraded when it's unable to be efficiently collected and assessed. (The board leadership should be kept in the loop on the progress of the study with appropriate reports made on process, timing, and outcomes.)

Third, as new indicators are identified it is necessary to do an in-depth review of how the information would be collected, consistency in policy application, timing for use and general points for reporting internally and publicly. There must be agreement on the use of the information by all parties. If, for example, it is determined that the system would like to provide annual reports on the progress of students being employed after graduation, then all must agree to how the data would be gathered and analyzed. It is possible that institutions would use different sources of information and in the process and provide outputs that weren't comparable. There would be little value in reporting such information to the public without an awareness that comparisons could not be made among institutions.

(Ultimately, if there are numerous new indicators that must be included in future analyses, then the process of developing and debating measures, from the system through each institution, becomes more complex. There must first be a consensus on the need for a new indicator and then a definition and source of data that will allow for collection. Similarly, it is critical there is a reassessment of existing indicators to be certain they are relevant to new reporting requirements.)

Fourth, the use of the information should be driven by its connection to answering key policy questions. It is important to know that a measure can be created and collected, but it should be done within the context of why it is needed. In any comprehensive review-of-information reporting requirements, some historical data will have little relevance in a new era and an updated system. There are many requirements in states that were mandated decades ago that no longer have any meaning in the current decision-making of the state but continue simply because they were mandated.

Fifth, the leadership of higher education at the system and institutional levels must fully agree to any requirements that are being added or altered as an outcome of the response to the governor. Invariably there will be varying impacts on each institution, and if there are anomalies, they should be understood by all. If there are expectations that institutions must take actions to enhance their reporting processes, definitions, or systems, then the timing and costs should be known to all as well. (Again, it is essential that the board leadership has been briefed on the progress of the study, particularly as they are close to offering a final approval—no surprises!)

Finally, once the institutions and system have reached agreement on the path moving forward, there should be a final review with the board. The board would have one last opportunity to make any changes it felt was necessary before sending a report the governor.

Ideally the chancellor with institutional presidents and board chair would personally deliver the information and go through the logic of the recommendations. (It is important to have given the governor's staff progress reports as well throughout the process—again no surprises!)

Connecting the Alternatives and SDMM

The use of the SDMM and planning and assessment framework give leaders the means through which they can look at large amounts of data and other input to construct alternatives. In this instance it was determined there would be one multipronged alternative. The choice of a single alternative didn't make the efforts any less valid but rather forced a broader inclusion of information that ensured all bases were touched.

We look through the questions of the P and A framework to develop alternatives for leadership consideration. While not directly discussed, the remaining components of the SDMM, particularly strategic thinking and the strategic planning process, give added context and support to various alternatives that are raised in the P and A framework. While we did not apply the full model, it should be understood that all six components should always in play.

CHAPTER 7

Institutional Leaders: Linking Local and System Goals

University and Community College Leader's Roles and Responsibilities

IF THE SYSTEM chancellor works with the greatest number of constituencies, institutional presidents have to attain the greatest depth on the widest range of issues. The number of issues confronted by an institution is compounded by complexity (i.e., vertical and horizontal levels of the organization and the necessary depth in exploring the implications of each issue). The system is interested in setting tuition and fees while the institution must break down the analysis into multiple levels of types of student and programs. Students are identified as graduate or undergraduate, resident or nonresident, degree-seeking or non-degree-seeking, international or not, on campus or off campus, and those taking course online. Other fees can be added by categories such as by discipline (engineering), by course (technology focused), and by degree (architecture). There are added groupings that get attention such as financial aid eligibility (based on economic status) and ethnicity. All the categories are analyzed through historical comparisons and specific peer comparisons to understand the composition of the overall student body and cost implications. The rigor to identify all potential implications of overlapping student categories requires strong data and planning mechanisms. The president must ensure the quality of the data and planning systems.

The institutional president must connect with students, faculty, staff, and academic and administrative leaders in a way that provides the greatest input, feedback, and follow-up on issues. They represent a constituent clearinghouse for leadership on virtually all issues. The job is to stimulate creative and strategic thinking on the part of his leadership team and others throughout the university or community college.

Governing Structure

A state board of higher education (or a similar functioning entity) in most states exists to provide leadership for public higher education. It is through the chancellor as the administrative connection to the board that institutional leaders receive their state-level direction. The institutions are governed through the board and in turn have their own structure based in part on the board's oversight and in part on their own capacity to govern.

In some states, universities have their own local boards that act as a preliminary stage in review and approval of information that is required by the state-level board. In some instances, the local board is more of a source for advocacy and less for in-depth critiquing of a universities proposed plans and strategies. In both cases, the institutional leader assumes significant responsibility for the agenda going to and flowing from the board's actions.

Interaction with Key Constituencies

The institutional president as suggested earlier must connect in some fashion with all constituencies—students, faculty, staff, boards, the legislature, governor's office, citizens of the state, and many more. There is no individual more aware of what is happening at the institution than its president. While the state board and chancellor will be apprised of key actions and directions of each system institution, they will not be involved with decision-making at the unit level. Thus, the institutional president is the first line of interaction with most constituencies. While there are many other leaders that will provide an institution's position on specific issues, the president is expected to have an awareness of all issues that are immediate, are of public concern, and have long range policy implications.

An important aspect of a president's role is interacting with the press. The press is a constituency that is always seeking to be informed on issues of both positive and negative consequence. The institution not only must respond to the press but do so with the attention to the conditions laid out by the board and chancellor. The implication of what occurs on a university and community college campus has ramifications for all public higher education. If there are protests by students on the carrying of guns on campus, then that will raise interest for the board and any existing policy it may have on gun safety. Each unit will have to respond to the public on their policies and how they allow or limit gun ownership on campus. If the use of guns gains prominence from an incident or injury, then the policies and means of enforcement become magnified. How the president coordinates the campus actions with the board and other units is of utmost importance.

Using the SDMM: Applying the Planning and Assessment Framework

Scenario

The board creates a state-level strategic plan extending out five years comprised of new and revised goals, priorities, and outcomes without attribution to specific targets on each campus. The board directs the chancellor to bring together all the institutions to fully explore the board mandates and how best to reach the system-level outcomes. The most obvious necessity, once all mandates by the board are understood, is to determine what the appropriate "share" of the system-level outcomes is for each university and community college. Embedded within the planning is the requirement to create a new funding model revolving around metrics connected to accountability measures. (Consider the same logic and need for the new funding model as in the scenario in chapter 6. The goal is to develop accountability measures as a product of the long-range strategic plan and build a funding model around those measures.)

Each institution must align its goals and priorities to those of the board. It must also assume its role in contributing quantitatively to those key indicators as targeted by the board. The chancellor should create alternative targets for each indicator by institution, which may be generated initially by each institution and modified after debate. Once the targets are agreed upon, which will be no easy task, the institutional presidents must create meaningful strategic plans that fully explore goals, priorities, and outcomes of the board. As would be expected each institution will have additional priorities and outcomes that align with their mission that must be incorporated into a comprehensive strategic plan.

Accountability or outcome measures can be found in most functional areas in higher education. The University of Wisconsin System has an annual report that has seven core strategies: preparing students, a stronger workforce, stronger businesses, stronger communities, resources, operational excellence, and collaborations (Kowan 2013). The seven core strategies are then broken down and measured through indicators. In this exercise, the higher education system must identify what they feel are the key indicators and link them to a funding model.

Planning and Assessment Framework

1. What is the problem? What creates instability? Is there
   agreement on the problem?

The most noteworthy problem is the demand by the board to reassess and rebuild institutional goals, priorities, programming, and outcomes in a manner that is measured periodically. The board objective is to get better information for their decision-making, information that is related to strategic plans and is measurable.

The state-level officials (governor and legislature) will use the information to make judgments about the viability of programs and their worthiness in receiving state support. The continuing expectation will be that if programs don't progress as planned and verified through objective measures, they may be reduced or eliminated. The problem becomes the potential misuse of information to make judgments not supported by the data.

Instability can come about from the uncertainty of how a new plan and process of measuring performance will affect institutional and departmental budgets. It is critical for institutional leaders to speak to the positive benefits of a new means of allocating funds based on a clear set of goals and outcomes.

One of the primary areas of attention by all constituencies will be on what happens if the targets or measures of performance are not attained. What are the disincentives for not reaching a given target? If budgets are reduced and there is constituency support for the programs, then the attention may be shifted to the accuracy or appropriateness of the indicators as a representative measure of the programs. The question will be raised as to the legitimacy of the indicator and not the value of the program.

If the program is not reaching its objective targets, then a question can be raised as to what intervening events have limited the success of the program. That is, if it was projected that enrollments would grow by 7% and they only grew by 3%, then were there unanticipated events such as an economic downturn, demographic shifts, or other disruptions that should have justifiably reduced the projections. (It is at this point that both internal and external constituents can represent the data from their own perspective to either support or cast doubt on success or failure.)

A different but related problem will be on the capacity of each institution to develop, track, and assess measures. Institutional leaders must be advocates for their programs and do everything they can to ensure they meet board goals. Thus, if some of the indicators are not easily captured it must be clear as to why that is the case and what will be done to substitute another measure as a willingness to be held accountable.

Each of the problems and related repercussions must be considered by the institutional president and team as new strategic directions tied to the measurement of key indicators are implemented. Not addressed at this point yet pivotal is the development of a new funding methodology tied to the outcome measures. Changing a funding methodology and redefining how money will be allocated can be extremely destabilizing. The president must lead in ensuring that all constituencies are aware of the ramifications of the planning and that they input into any of the planning processes.

2. What examples contribute to the problem? What is the
   magnitude of the problem?

The problem of redefining an institution in a short period of time and in a manner that forces acknowledgment that some existing programs and services aren't addressing current expectations is daunting. There may be an acceptance of change that adds to an institutions program inventory and is positive but little incentive to reduce programs and services. The challenge for all is to embrace the board's new directions and realistically recalibrate programs to not only match the new directions but also determine how current plans fit into a new future. The inability of institutional leadership to make honest attempts to present alternatives that would negatively impact some campus programs and services is often a cause for dismissal.

The severity of the problem or in this instance the difficulty of reprogramming institutional plans and funding methods will be seen in the degree to which constituencies support the outcomes of a process. If the process defines new program directions and funding strategies that are not in line with their expectations, then they will feel threatened. The potential loss of funds creates more instability in an institution than most any other problem. The magnitude of the problem worsens if the process is not transparent, well communicated, and built on input from constituencies that in the end were disadvantaged.

3. What is the origin of the current examples of the problem? What caused the problem?

The board's mandate for an overhaul of the system and institutional goals, priorities, and outcomes is the basis for current efforts for change. It may have come from new board leadership representing a changing view of the board membership. It may have been because the existing plans had not been reassessed for years and not reflective of current program, demographic, and financial conditions.

The likely foundation of the mandate is to better define and address the future demands for public higher education. There is a desire to be ahead of change through proactive planning and action.

4. Is there a historical precedent for the problem? Does the precedent connect with current issues?

Public boards throughout the country over the last fifteen years have been asking their units to adapt to state-funding cuts. The most common way has been to take a much closer look at programs after clearly outlining organizational goals, strategic directions, desired outcomes, and potential costs. It is the institutional president and leadership staff that must translate system expectations into institutional plans.

The lesson learned by institutional leaders is how to work through the system-led planning process and gain maximum benefit for the university or college. If leaders can gain the trust of their chancellor and board, they can be actively influencing decisions to their benefit. The precedents of prior planning processes and outcomes offers leader's experiences that help avoid any possible pitfalls.

5. Which constituencies are most affected? Do all constituencies feel there is a problem? What is the relative stake for each?

The movement of a system and institution away from accepted norms (existing strategic directions) into potentially very different directions affects all constituencies. The institutional president is charged with the responsibility of leading the institution with guidance from the system/chancellor while having managerial freedom and flexibility. The leadership must have direct involvement and ongoing support from students, faculty, and staff. The process must be transparent and be shared with the governor's office, the legislature, and the public at large.

The magnitude of change in quantity and quality is such that all constituencies are affected. How much they are impacted is dependent on the type, degree, and timing of change. The type of change gives a further sense of which constituencies are most at risk and those that may benefit. If the institution is putting greater emphasis on programs that are more business related and less on social sciences, that will create more concern for faculty and students in the social sciences. If the objective is to raise student tuition to specific standard and that will mean increases over the next x number of years, then the students will argue. If it is determined that the institution will reallocate funds from the library to support academic counseling programs, it will be viewed as detrimental to the library and get some negative attention.

In the end, if the institutional leadership uses information from discussion and debate gained from open forums and communicates widely and in a transparent fashion, then the eventual decisions will be driven from processes that recognized most if not all constituencies. That is of importance in that all constituencies have a stake in the outcomes. The fact that a constituency had some funding reallocated to another program at least will have come out of open discussions.

6. Provide alternatives or actions on how to strategically prepare for and address similar examples in the future.

The institutional president must first take the lead from the board and chancellor as to the structure, timing, and outcomes expected from the processes at the system level. In turn, the president must build, with consultation of key constituencies, processes that incorporates the existing institutional goals and priorities and assesses their relevance against the future expectations as driven through rigorous strategic planning and decision-making processes. While current goals and priorities represent a jump off point or baseline, they should be modified or readapted as future expectations dictate change.

It would be very risky for a president to move too far afield of board-level guidance in building a strategic plan. However, it is also incumbent on the institutional leadership to be advocates for their programs and offer alternatives that better reflect their institutional programs as generally represented by system goals or priorities.

In advance of developing alternatives, let's summarize the conditions confronted by public higher education as posed by the board. Below are the assumptions:

- The board mandates a new strategic plan extending out five years.
- The plan will reassess all goals, strategies, priorities, and outcomes in creating a performance-based analysis
- Institutions will create plans modeled off the system goals.
- Institutions will create measures consistent with the system plan and in aggregate will achieve the system-level targets for various measures.
- The chancellor will lead the effort with particular attention paid to assigning the appropriate "share" of system wide goals to each institution.
- A new funding model will be developed linked to the performance measures.

Alternatives

Alternative 1: In a perfect world there would be a set of targets for universities and community colleges within a system of higher education that could be broken into "shares" that accurately portrayed the wishes of each institution and aggregated into the goal of the system target. A target at the system level for full-time enrollments might be two hundred thousand, with each university and community contributing their fair share. What happens if an institution provides a target that the chancellor and board feels is less than they should be doing (i.e., feels less based on historical data or perception of growth into the future)?

It is particularly noteworthy because the system goal may not be met if one or more institutions are unable to grow as expected. The institutional leadership must then negotiate for the number they feel is reasonable based on program growth, demographics, cost implications, etc. The essence of negotiations is to determine if there is room for compromise and what the implications are for other institutions in the system. Do other universities pick up the difference and assume a greater burden or do they step back and suggest they have reached their limit in growth? Does the system downsize its estimates to fit the individual targets?

In this alternative, it is assumed there is sufficient compromise that allows for reaching the system target as set by the board with other institutions picking up the slack.

If we take the enrollment as one measure and are developing an addition twenty-five to forty accountability measures, it can be seen very quickly that the capacity of the collective set of institutions in the system will not always be able to meet the targets set by their board. Assuming that is the case, then compromise and cooperation is paramount.

Alternative 2: Let us assume that an institution can't reach a research funding target set by the board, and it is seen as a critical shortfall for the system. The system is not interested in accommodating the institution and seeks a separate analysis that confirms that their target can't be reached. (This is less a major alternative for a system but rather example of how differences between the system and an institution would have to be resolved prior to arriving at a final plan.)

At this point, the institutional president and board have taken positions that are in opposition to one another. The president must present the program goals, plans, data, and accountability measures that support the institutional case. If the case is convincing, then members of the board may be able to some compromise. If not, it is more likely the president will have to accept board recommendations or look for other employment. While it may sound extreme, there are presidents representing their constituencies on issues viewed as the core of their future that, when in conflict with their board, must take stands that passionately support that future.

In this instance, to end on a positive, the board gained a better understanding of the institutions research goals particularly the drop in funding at the federal level. A reduction dictated by future projections, changes in the types of research, and positive growth seen in out years (beyond the five-year plan), and generally, logic was clearly constructed and presented in a manner convincing to the board and the public. The board revised their system target overall and did not ask other institutions to revise their targets upward.

Final Thoughts

Cooperation and compromise allowed all parties to feel positive about their positions and the direction moving forward. The interactions were largely among internal constituencies and focused on little-p politics. Once plans move into the external environment with a wider visibility, including the governor, the public, and the legislature, there would be positive and negative reactions. If, as an example the system decided to grow substantially beyond current levels in students it could have impacts on facilities, financing, tuition, fees, etc. If those implications were assuming greater state funding, then there would be immediate reaction from the governor's office and the legislature. If the plans suggested a cutback in students served, then there would be concern raised by the public regarding their access to a public higher education. If there were to be an elimination of academic programs, then the advocates for those programs would be lobbying to the legislature and governor seeking their support to intervene. In turn, the governor and legislature would be requesting more detailed information on the initiatives proposed and their rationale for termination.

The internal and external arenas for debate and action will always have constituencies that are opposed on given issues. The same constituencies may be aligned on other issues. In the long run there is a need to cooperate to the greatest extent possible and maintain positive relationships and offer periodic communications with both internal and external parties. It is inevitable that what goes around comes around thus it is useful to compromise on issues today where you can gain value on future negotiations.

Connecting the Alternatives and SDMM

The use of the SDMM in support of the board's expectations for a strategic plan extending out five years would be the best example of its application. The institutions could work in concert with the system and one another without feeling the pressures and instability created by processes mandated by externa constituencies. The full application of strategic thinking, a comprehensive strategic planning process, and the use of the P and A framework in conjunction with using the best historical and future-looking data could be done under more controlled and thoughtful transparent processes.

The outcomes would be vital for institutions as related to how they would measure success and be funded based on performance. However, the creation of the five-year plan and accompanying accountability structure would be done in a way managed by the system without external coercion or expectations.

CHAPTER 8

Students as Consumers Individually and Collectively

STUDENTS ARE OFTEN viewed as some relatively homogenous group of people attending a college or university. You often hear questions posed like how do students feel about safety on campus or time to graduate or resident halls quality or financial aid availability? The answers of course vary greatly depending on the type of student you are: Are you a resident or nonresident student, international student, scholarship student, fraternity or sorority member, part-time or full-time student, undergraduate or graduate student? Are you in the band, ROTC, or athletics? And so on.

The collective nature of a student body consists of numerous categories that a student may have multiple memberships. A band member may have a scholarship, is a full-time student, may be a resident of the state, and is an undergraduate. Given the potential permutations of the overlapping memberships, it is clear that there is no singular homogenous group representing all students.

Governing Structures

Millions of students attend an institution under the oversight of a state board of higher education. They are subject to the expectations of a board as translated broadly through a system chancellor and more specifically through the institutional president. It is at the institutional level that they realize their greatest opportunities for influencing their own agendas.

The nature of internal student governance is that students form into an independent government that is closely connected to the university administrative organization and related processes. There are multiple student committees that support specific student issues and, in some cases, act as conduits to the university administration. Student leadership works with the university leaders in both understanding university expectations but also sharing concerns raised by students that may take some input and action by the university. They seek to understand the fairness of actions by university administrators. The most notable action is the annual tuition increases and the value derived to the students. What new programs or services, if any, are as a result of their added tuition? Depending on their conclusions of fairness and value, they work with the institutional leadership to seek possible alternatives that better address student priorities. If tuition increases are approved how will the students benefit? Are more classes offered to accelerate graduation? Are technology enhancements expanded? Are support services such as academic counseling expanded? Will there be more limited cost increases in the future? And so on. Ultimately, there is dialogue that offers all sides a forum and, in many instances, acknowledges mutual willingness to work out differences. Compromise is a key factor.

Interaction with Key Constituencies

Students are the key stakeholders in higher education and as a consequence do interact with all constituencies. They interact with one another in governing themselves on academic and administrative issues. Their capacity to influence decisions beyond their own governance rests with the avenues of communications and actions afforded by their institution. While they do have access to board meetings, their primary pathway to voicing their opinions is with their institutional president, financial leadership, student affairs leadership, and others, as designated, on given organizational issues. The most prominent role typically is offering input on new academic programs, offering advice on budget issues impacting their lives, providing alternative tuition and fee increase recommendations, originating initiatives on resident halls, seeking expanded financial aid opportunities, etc.

Perhaps the most obvious role as mentioned earlier is working with the administration on tuition and fee increases. They are concerned not only about the magnitude of an increase but as importantly how the funds are to be used. Do they gain a direct benefit from the increase? Or will they simply be applied against a loss in state funds and only act to continue existing programs. Is additional financial aid available to help offset the increase?

The students seek and offer input on academic programs that may be added or terminated as suggested by faculty. They will suggest potential changes to technology used by faculty in classroom settings.

Students will provide their input on key issues identified by the institution to the governor, the legislature, and in other public forums. While they do not have a major ongoing role in external presentations, they can be very convincing when giving their thoughts and opinions. The public can be a very important ally with students as they can combine to offer very real and emotional arguments on the implications of costs on student's ability to attend an institution. There is nothing more compelling than parents speaking about their son's or daughter's inability to identify funds to begin or continue attendance at a university or community college or the tremendous burden in assuming substantial amounts of debt to attend.

Using the SDMM: Applying the Planning and Assessment Framework

Scenario

The state legislature reduces the higher education state funding by 6%. They also place restrictions on how the funding can be used (i.e., no new programs unless they drive verifiable economic development opportunities). They offer increased flexibility through limiting reporting requirements to other state agencies. System and institutions will spend less time and resources on tracking, analyzing, and reporting information that is considered duplicative or no longer required.

Higher Education Response

The university president has asked students to absorb a 10% increase in tuition in the upcoming year as part of a plan to address major reductions by the state. The 10% increase will be felt across all student categories and will drive few if any new benefits in student programs. The increase is simply to offset state-funding losses. The students have lobbied for limited tuition increases but also expanded course availability, upgraded labs, clearer paths to career opportunities, and increased involvement in university decision-making.

The state-funding reductions have averaged 8% annually over the last three years. The students have had tuition increases averaging 7% over the same time period. The faculty has had one 3% compensation increase during those same three years. Needless to say, all constituencies are concerned about the compound effect of reductions going forward.

Planning and Assessment Framework

1. What is the problem? What creates instability? Is there
   agreement on the problem?

The loss of funding from the state drives the pain of downsizing decision-making from the state to the system to the university. The loss of funding and growing tuition has severely affected the students and faculty confidence in the state and university. There are continuing demands for forums to reassess leadership decisions and seek answers that will suggest alternative solutions. Unfortunately, any alternative will have constituencies that benefit more than others (i.e., there are always winners and losers). Thus, the primary catalyst of state-funding cuts creates a myriad of other problems for all constituencies.

There is growing instability for all constituencies as reductions have become commonplace over the last three years. Students have had to assume the role as primary source of funding through tuition and fees and not realized any programmatic enhancements from the added funds. They agree there is a problem but feel that they shouldn't be as large a part of the solution as they have been and will be in the upcoming year.

2. What examples contribute to the problem? What is the
   magnitude of the problem?

The primary problem is the continuing loss of state funds. The loss is chronic and left academic and administrative programs in state of disarray. The capacity to find new funds falls substantially to students through added tuition and fees. The students feel disenfranchised. In effect there is a cycle of diminishing state support (financially and programmatically) that seems to have little potential for slowing down. To worsen the situation, there is little appetite on the part of many states to see public higher education as a key public good and higher priority.

The severity or difficulty of the problem is the compounded nature of reductions over many years. The sense of instability and uncertainty grows from year to year. For the students they have had to pay more money, seek added financial aid, and see growing time to degree in graduation.

3. What is the origin of the current examples of the problem? What caused the problem?

The loss of state funds has been a routine occurrence for three years. The loss of funds has been both real and artificial. State government in most states realized major revenue losses during the great recession beginning in 2008. However, prior to 2008 and since gaining some ground from 2015 and beyond, most states have maintained low tax rates as a political big-P promise for reasons of ideology and self-preservation.

There is little change on the horizon for state support, and as has been the case, the students continue to pay higher tuition and fee costs. From an institutional standpoint the potential of not attracting new students and losing existing students is very real, which is a major factor for any program and funding decisions.

4. Is there a historical precedent for the problem? Does the precedent connect with current issues?

Beyond the three-year period of reduced state funds and increased tuition there have been no appreciable increases for a decade. Prior to the great recession, there was a lessened value placed on public higher education as governments chose to reduce taxes and limit services to state residents.

As state funds have declined the system turned to students for an increasing commitment in tuition and fees.

Historical precedent is directly connected to current issues. There has been a continuing decline in state funds and denial of any new funds to public higher education as an answer to state priorities. The action of higher education in response to decline has been to increase tuition and fees, which has diminishing returns over time. Students can make other educational choices that will limit their financial burden and still gain employment.

5. Which constituencies are most affected? Do all constituencies feel there is a problem? What is the relative stake for each?

The students are the constituency most affected. They pay higher tuition and fees while feeling the reduction in course availability, fewer faculties to teach courses, and growing time to degree pressure (and related costs). The faculty continues to be undercompensated by peer standards and bear the brunt of downsizing in numbers of faculty and courses. Institutional leadership seeks answers to stem the tide of degraded programs and services but must rethink strategies regularly to meet changing expectations.

The public is split on its support for public higher education (and other state priorities). One segment of citizens views public higher education from the standpoint of its educational, economic, and social value to the state. They see a benefit collectively to the well-being of the state. There is another segment that suggests they don't want to pay higher taxes to support residents and that if a resident wants a higher education, they should pay for it. They see the downside in terms of the costs they bear individually. In a sense, it is akin to the argument of many paying for health care or insurance covering a large population knowing that not all people will necessarily get sick and require a higher level of insurance.

6. Provide alternatives or actions on how to strategically prepare for and address similar examples in the future.

There are a number of directions students can take when creating alternatives responding to the scenario they confront. There best chance for success is gaining support from other constituencies. Depending on the issues and levels of competition not all constituencies will support one another. Students have less institutional governing authority and as a consequence must seek to influence others to support their causes. Thus, their internal role and relationship with the institutional leadership, governing board, and faculty is paramount in advancing their positions.

In advance of developing alternatives, let's summarize the conditions confronted by public higher education as posed by the governor and legislature.

- The state is recommending reductions of 6%—this follows 24% cuts over the prior three years.
- There has been continuing loss of state funds over the last three years specifically but there is a longer history of downsizing and neglect prior to the 2008 recession.
- The president is recommending a 10% increase in tuition and fees.
- Students have assumed the role of offsetting state-funding losses with added tuition and fees—2% increase over the three prior years.
- Faculty members have not been compensated adequately, relative to peers, for years.
- The state will limit administrative guidelines and reporting requirements to give some flexibility and potential savings to institutions

Alternatives

Alternative 1: The students decide to align themselves entirely with the communications strategies (e.g., lobbying efforts of the system and their institution). In so doing, they realize that their primary objective of limiting tuition and fees is not the highest priority. They feel that if they can be seen as productive partners in the processes that they may gain some advantage. Also, if there are any changes in the amount of funds cut by the legislature, that may reduce the 10% tuition increase target set by the institution. The pathway is through cooperation which may eventually lead to compromise or a softening of the institutional position on tuition.

It is also an intention of the students to maximize their visibility with all constituencies. They want to participate in any public forums that speak to institutional needs and convey student's priorities. They seek the ability to make formal presentations that outline the impacts of statewide reductions from the student perspective.

Students speaking to faculty groups such as faculty senates highlighting the negative impacts on student participation and student programming can be powerful. The escalating tuition costs and lowered state funding creates disruptions in student access, numbers and types of degree programs, counseling services, etc., all of which have direct linkages to faculty service. Connecting students as the core constituency that faculty serve can bring about closer alliances and benefit students in the eyes of institutional leadership. It becomes even more productive when the students and faculty can make joint statements that further their support for one another and the institutional and statewide higher education agenda.

Public forums such as board meetings provide one of the best opportunities to express concerns and priorities in a setting that has statewide attention. System and institutional leaders create a statewide agenda and strategies in a setting that clarifies to the entire state their distress with recommendations that continue to degrade public higher education. The students can be active participants in corroborating their sense of loss in both objective and subjective terms.

Such meetings can be used as a bully pulpit for the entire state to experience. The students must hope that the approach brings visibility to their concerns but also does not too aggressively attack the governor.

Lobbying is the natural extension of higher education taking its case to the key external constituencies of the governor and legislature. The legislative hearings, meetings with the governor and meetings with legislators become all-consuming requirements for each institution and the system leadership including board members. In this alternative, it is essential that students be able to market their concerns from a constituent perspective but with attention to the system wide goals and priorities.

This alternative is the most common over time in pulling together all higher education constituencies into as united a front as possible. While there are always outliers who feel disenfranchised by a lack of representation the majority are supportive. If things go as hoped, the approach would offer some relief on the magnitude of state reduction, the students could benefit from a lower tuition increase and some technology enhancement, faculty may receive a small compensation increase, and there would be some goodwill among all for the collective efforts of all. On the flip side, if reductions held as recommended, there would be a cascading effect of further loss by all constituencies and future relationships may be eroded. The implications for the future may be a sense that it is better to act more aggressively and not completely connected to system and institutional coat tails.

Alternative 2: The students feel that they must align themselves with the system and institutional priorities but are seeking greater representation in public and private forums. They want to be able to tell their side of the story unfettered by brief time limits for presentation. Explanations in some depth on diminished access, loss of degree program options, growing time to degree impacts, cost escalation, and perceived quality loss takes time to accurately understand their plight. In essence, they don't want to be seen as an insignificant component in a wider system or institutional agenda.

It is the intent to establish more forums within the institution to generate student awareness and support for their collective cause. Building coalitions on key issues and creating their own lobbying efforts beyond the system-led approach is necessary. Isolating specific students that can speak articulately to the issues as advocates and work with their local legislative representatives is one tool in lobbying.

Another tool is for students to seek broader public support by canvassing communities with the story of historical losses, implications for current students, and the uncertainty of public higher education going into the future. They must give their story with personal anecdotes of loss, fear of loss, and continuing uncertainty.

As suggested in alternative 1, the students should work as closely as possible with the faculty in driving home the absolute connection of teacher and student. While they may not be engaged in all lobbying efforts, they can still create some joint meetings with legislators and highlight their united approach in the substance of higher education concerns and solutions.

The risk for students in taking a greater role in lobbying is that it may not fit the system or institutional approach and appear to offer different priorities. Confusion can be an outcome of uncoordinated lobbying efforts. If students and leadership can be pitted against one another, they all lose. Students in the long run could be even bigger losers if they are perceived as having hurt any opportunities for addbacks. The system and university leadership could make tuition increases a bit easier by being able to place some of the blame directly on the students. Ultimately, alternative 2 is a second option of choice. However, as financial fortunes for higher education continue to dwindle and students are asked to pay a higher and higher percentage of the cost of an education, alternative 2 begins to look more reasonable.

Connecting the Alternatives and SDMM

The SDMM and planning assessment framework should provide the vehicles through which leaders can assess the value of alternatives 1 and 2. It may be that there is a hybrid through which students are closely coordinating with leadership in the system lobbying and being given a greater, more individual role in their own lobbying efforts. The assessment may be that students should have a greater role given their stake as the primary "customer" of the higher education enterprise. The role would be greater depth and exposure in meetings to discuss their goals and priorities, but also clearly aligned with the priorities of the institution and system.

Faculty: Individual and Collective Value to Higher Education

Individual Roles

FACULTY REPRESENTS THE primary point of contact between a student and their respective community college or university. Faculty members are the face of the institution to students. The institution has a primary goal of providing instruction to students as a means of bettering the opportunities for employment, advancement in a position, growth in a desired discipline, or simply enjoyment of a given topic of interest. It is each faculty member's responsibility to create a positive environment for student learning in all its forms.

Like each student there isn't a single model or prototype of an ideal faculty member. Within the context of a diverse educational environment, there are countless ways for students to learn and faculty to teach.

Governing Structures/Committees

While faculty governing structures vary throughout institutional settings nationally they have processes, which like student government, features aspects of independence in governing, and in some instances is directly connected into the university decision-making structure. Ultimately, faculty has the opportunity to debate issues that concern themselves, students, and the university.

In many institutions there is a body of faculty, often called faculty senate, which represents the faculty as a whole. It is constructed to offer a deliberative resource that focuses on the role of the faculty in not only teaching and research but also in the administrative directions of the institution. They work within their charter to guide and benefit all faculty members but also offer advice and recommendations to the university leadership. As the constituency that is most visible in delivering the primary "product" (of instruction), the faculty concerns are always important to the broader university administration.

They reflect, through various committees, attention to concerns for the quality of instructional programs, availability of classes for high interest disciplines, compensation equity, program planning, accreditation processes, implications of state mandates on work, research versus instruction workloads, and other institutional issues. They provide a collective position on institutional facility needs, compensation for all employees, student tuition and fees, efficiency opportunities, employability of students graduating from academic programs, etc.

Interaction with Key Constituencies

The faculty interacts, most frequently and intensely, with students. It is their primary function to give instruction and guidance on an ongoing basis to the benefit of the student. They teach courses and also advise on program and career opportunities. An individual faculty member may have more influence over the decision of a student in the career choice than any other factor. That is, while they may not suggest a student become an accountant or a lawyer, they can give guidance on a career path as outlined through college degree programs. They can also counsel a student on the specific course "value" or relevance of a given profession, suggest the "fit" for a student's academic capacity and desire, and as importantly, offer options that guide a student's decisions.

They work with the institutional leadership in expressing their opinions on topics that have implications for specific areas and the institution as a whole. They can work with the leadership in bringing forward key initiatives and ideas to the state. As the thought leaders of their given disciplines, they can sit on local, state, and federal committees as expert consultants. The state has responsibilities for economic development, infrastructure, public safety, health and human services, corrections, etc., all areas that universities and community colleges possess experts in their fields.

Ultimately, faculty members individually and collectively are more than just teachers and researchers. They bring a keen awareness and extraordinary knowledge on important topics for all state citizens. They teach our teachers in K-12, the engineers who build roads and buildings, the farmers who use the newest technology in feeding the US, the business leaders who support the economy, the governmental leaders who make critical decisions for our welfare, and almost every other category that supports the American lifestyle.

Using the SDMM: Applying the Planning and Assessment Framework

Scenario

The governor is recommending a reduction in the state budgets of 5% in each year of an upcoming biennium. The reductions represent the third biennia in a row for cuts. The governor is asking for a new strategic statewide plan from the board and each institution that expects cuts in the number of faculty and staff. Also, student enrollments must be at least maintained at current levels but with some possible incentives to increase access. The goal is to increase efficiency in the delivery of programs and services. The system can raise the tuition and fees but with acknowledgment of maintaining access for residents of the state. The governor supports strategic goals and action that will enhance economic development initiatives that benefit the state.

The legislature will likely follow the governor's lead but is less concerned about how the system reduces budgets (e.g., targeting faculty and staff) and more about the bottom-line savings.

Higher Education Response

The chancellor of the system works with institutional leaders to create a planning process and guidance on the process. The board will offer a statewide perspective on the vision for the future higher-education goals, key initiatives, accountability measures (targets to be determined through the review), and general expectations regarding process timing, transparency, and constituent involvement. Each institution will replicate the planning outline of the board but with attention to their local or statewide mission. The chancellor will work with the institutional leaders who in turn will work with their own constituencies like the faculty and students.

There will be an attempt to create communications strategies that organize discussions and outcomes with input from the faculty. The goal will be to gain as much consensus as possible when taking the strategic plan to the governor. The same process will be used with students and other academic and administrative representatives. Ultimately, the intent is to gain as much agreement on goals, outcomes, and general positioning with the board vision from all institutions and constituencies.

Planning and Assessment Framework

1. What is the problem? What creates instability? Is there agreement on the problem?

The state continues to reduce funding support but now with conditions. They expect to reduce the number of faculty and staff while increasing efficiency. They also mandate no impact on student access. The system and institutions will have to document their responses to the governor's mandate through a multiyear strategic plan.

The explicit requirement to reduce faculty and staff is the primary focus for the leadership and faculty. Instability is a logical outcome of the recommendations. A broad-based reduction of 5% per year for two years compounded by prior years neglect will affect all constituencies.

Perhaps the requirement for a strategic plan will offer some avenues for higher education to present a case that recognizes the benefits of support of public higher education.

2. What examples contribute to the problem? What is the magnitude of the problem?

As in all the scenarios, the predicate is the state decision to pull funding from state programs. Other factors flowing from the main problem are the historical loss of funds compounded by the new reductions, the implications of further losses on program and institutional accreditation, questions of quality, student access, inability to attract and retain key faculty, etc. The list of examples generated by the continuing drawdown of state funds grows in magnitude of program impacts as the state commitment diminishes annually.

The identification of faculty and staff as specific targets for cutbacks, along with the restriction on student enrollments, and expectations for increased efficiency and growing economic development place higher education in an impossible position. The severity of the problems for all constituencies, but most pointedly for the faculty, is at the highest level.

3. What is the origin of the current examples of the problem? What caused the problem?

While the previous two biennia reflect drops in state funding the actual origin can be traced back to earlier times prior to and during the great recession. The historical context suggests that there were attempts to lower state taxes and therein reduce funding driven into state coffers. Until the last fifteen years the attempts were generally met with some resistance that produced minor periodic reductions. However, as states took on more conservative leadership the ability to move state taxes lower became more commonplace in many states. In 2008, the great recession brought a more permanent necessity to reduce funding based on the dramatic drop in state taxes. The continuation of the recession memorialized the sense that taxpayers could or would not support higher taxes, and as a consequence, programs were terminated or cut severely to adjust to the new normal.

4. Is there a historical precedent for the problem? Does the precedent connect with current issues?

The three biennia represent evidence of state-funding cutbacks. However, as suggested in question 3, there had been downsizing of programs going back to before 2008 and the great recession. The decisions by state leaders to reduce funding support had been based on both fiscal exigency and ideology. The extreme nature of the recession allowed for legislative actions that would not have been acted on in more moderate or financially secure times.

The leadership lesson should have been to be prepared with alternative solutions that assumed further losses in state funds and growing tuition and fees. Assuming there are some plans in place, leaders can consider those as they assess how to respond to the governor. The existing plans may fall short of what is needed programmatically and financially. If the plans did recognize potential losses in state funds at the levels recommended (which should have been the basis for state plans in recent years), then there would be an accompanying set of revised goals, altered programs, and new outcomes that either identify new funds to offset state cuts or scenarios that did reduce faculty and staff.

If the plans were not in place, then the process of creating new strategies in concert with all constituent expectations is markedly more difficult. If realignment plans did not exist, it offers an opportunity to rethink and redefine a new form and approach to higher education. It may, out of necessity, be very different and create student learning opportunities that are more adaptable to current economic conditions. The precedent of the loss of funding will move beyond typical reduction options and tuition increases to a wholly different means of developing and delivering programs and services.

5. Which constituencies are most affected? Do all constituencies feel there is a problem? What is the relative stake for each?

All constituencies are impacted by the continuing loss of funds. In this scenario the burden falls particularly hard on faculty and staff. The governor has offered specific conditions that would cut faculty and staff without any sense of potential compromise.

Again, the loss in state funds is simply compounding over multiple biennia with few choices left from which leaders can make decisions that don't severely affect all constituencies. If the decision is to increase tuition and fees to offset some of the loss, then student access may be limited, debt increased, and time to graduation lengthened. If it is decided to eliminate degree programs to meet the faculty cut, then students have fewer choices and the institution loses programs that had been important.

Under any circumstance the targeting of faculty creates uncertainty and instability among the faculty and leadership as they create strategic efforts to maintain the core of the institution, its instructional programs.

All constituencies have much at stake. A comprehensive plan will eventually define the overall revised goals and strategies of each institution and include the actions on faculty reductions, tuition increases, and enrollment estimates that will clarify the relative stakes of each constituency.

6. Provide alternatives or actions on how to strategically prepare for and address similar examples in the future.

The focus of this set of alternatives is on faculty. How do leaders make decisions that are based on the new funding levels and meeting key system and institutional goals? Perhaps a silver lining is the mandate that higher education must develop a strategic plan to address the governor's expectations. However, it can also can be a tool to recast and remarket the goals and values of higher education. It is a vehicle to offer new ideas and initiatives that can reinvigorate higher education while also highlighting its value to the state. It can redefine why moving forward into the future requires a more robust higher education for the state and its residents.

In advance of developing alternatives, let's summarize the conditions confronted by public higher education as posed by the governor. The conditions are unusually restrictive and limit higher education's flexibility in dealing with downsizing. Below are the assumptions:

- The governor recommends reducing state funds by 5% annually in the upcoming biennium.
- The funding cuts represent the third consecutive biennium of reductions.
- The plan must reduce faculty and staff numbers as one response to loss of funding.
- The plan should create a more efficient means of developing and delivering programs and services
- Initiatives should be introduced that bolster state economic development activities.
- Student enrollments should be maintained with an emphasis on retaining and attracting state residents.
- Tuition and fees can be increased but not to the extent that enrollments are negatively affected.
- The legislature is in general agreement with the governor's mandate but is less concerned about whether or not the faculty or the staff is reduced.
- A multiyear strategic plan for the system and for each institution must be presented.

Alternatives

Alternative 1: The reduction of faculty raises a number of critical issues that must be addressed by leaders. Should faculty members be terminated in small numbers cutting across many disciplines? If so, what is the impact on the instructional offerings in each discipline and is the affect to downgrade quality over many programs? If they are taken from a limited number of disciplines, are the academic programs in jeopardy of not being viable? If so, which ones are the least valued by the academic leadership? Once chosen how many students are impacted? What are the tenure rights for faculty that are terminated? What are the costs for paying faculty severance pay or any other benefits that might be contractually required?

The complexity of program eliminations and terminating faculty does require an institution wide assessment of all programs, relative values in addressing the institutional mission, and existing strategic plans and positions. It is always preferable to find programs that aren't considered as valuable in the context of student instruction and counseling as a first point of reduction. Unfortunately, after years of loss, there are few less-essential, nonacademic programs available as low hanging fruit.

The system chancellor must first create a process that all institutions will comply with in addressing the governor's mandate. The chancellor would have conversations with the board and institutional leaders to define approaches in first meeting the governor's expectations. There should be agreement on the specific expectations from the board as translated through the chancellor to each institution. Consistency in process, timing, and substance is critical.

It is as important to seize the opportunity to create a plan that accurately reflected the vision and desired directions over the next five years and beyond. While the governor may have intended the plan to limit higher education's program growth, it can be a vehicle to fully define its value to the public and be more than a document of subtraction and loss. It could and should be a process marked with constituent debate on all issues eventually translated into a set of strategies that leaders use to market and lobby for a "new" public higher education.

From a purely process related standpoint each institution would follow the overall guidelines of the board but have flexibility to create options that best suited their current and future plans. It is through the individual institutions that creative solutions would emerge, including how leaders could advocate for faculty.

In this alternative, the number of faculty and related programs to be cut is reviewed by the chancellor and institutional leaders. The purpose is to begin to develop a rationale for reductions with the intent of identifying as few as possible. Perhaps even making the case for a revised reduction plan less than what the governor has suggested. Criteria on programs by institution, enrollments by discipline, faculty tenure, potential academic programs that could be downsized, and implications for future programming would be reviewed consistently as it cuts across all institutions. One of the key necessities of good planning is being consistent in dealing with issues that affect all institutions. If one institution can apply a different set of factors in determining tenure, program quality, compensation, etc., those differences should be known when decisions are made. The worst outcome in any planning endeavor is arriving at a point when decisions are made and discover that the variables used to make judgments about program or individual viability differ across institutions.

The academic and administrative leadership at each institution should work with the deans and department heads in clarifying the implications of the governor's recommendations, the guidance provided by the board and the goals and process of the president. There should be no doubt in what the goals are from the standpoint of the governor's recommendations and as translated by system and chancellor.

The faculty at each institution should actively engage their leadership with ideas that help structure the conversations about academic programming. They must work through their faculty senates in organizing processes of debate that will inform themselves, institutional leadership, and external constituencies. It must be clear what the job of being a faculty member includes teaching, research/

discovery, counseling, advising, community consulting, and writing. There are many tasks that define faculty members and any response to the governor and the public should indicate what is lost to individual students, the institution, community, and state when a faculty member is terminated.

The academic leaders must lead in reassessing the capacity of their departments, colleges, and other units to adequately meet their most basic ongoing missions. If the program assessment and strategic planning processes indicates a major makeover, then academic leadership must be the primary source in influencing the timing and shape of any realignment. The implications of the changes for student access, program availability, time to graduation, etc., must be clear. The recommendations made by academic leaders will be as influential in setting the future programming as any constituency but will be woven into the overall redefinition of all institutional programming. As each institution completes their plan, the chancellor should be working with leadership to digest all the inputs to ensure the overall goals set out by the governor and the more-enhanced goals of the board have been addressed. As mentioned earlier, consistency is very important. If one institution goes beyond system goals without some prior discussion and prior approval, then other institutions will feel they have been cheated. There isn't anything more difficult to contain than presidents who feel the system/board has allowed some advantage to one institution that takes away from their request. It can lead to off the books attempts to lobby either for initiatives not approved by the board or lobbying against an initiative that the system didn't fully address in its goals. Ill feelings will continue for years. The faculty must continue to do their job even after recommendations move to the board and the strategic plan is sent to the governor; they must continue regardless of the long-term implications of program realignment.

They should be a key component in selling the new strategies to the public. If there are losses in faculty, they should speak to how the future will be different and give positive thoughts under the new plan. There is no reason to dwell on what was lost or point fingers at leaders that they felt did not do enough to defend their programs.

Once the plan has moved from the board to the governor and legislature, there should be active efforts by each institution in conjunction with the system/chancellor to market the new plan. They should lobby constituencies outside of higher education to both educate and advocate for the new directions. If the governor or legislature relents on their initial recommendations for higher education, then there may be an increase in funding or flexibility from which to react to the upcoming years. If the legislature doesn't addback any funds, higher education will still have a new plan which strengthens all constituency knowledge of what the future holds and, in particular for the faculty, provide a realigned blueprint for goals, objectives, workloads, and other student centric options. The plan will be a resource to review by the system and each institution when developing program plans, enrollment projections, budgets, and other information on an ongoing basis. It represents a source of continuity that helps both internal and external constituencies understand their commitments in meeting the agreed-upon goals and how successful they are in supporting student and state expectations. There is point in looking backward as difficult as that might be.

Alternative 2: The second alternative differs from the first by the way in which it is marketed to the governor, the legislature, and the public. The first option put more emphasis on working as positively as possible with external constituencies. The idea was to gain support through cooperation and understanding and less through confrontation and divisive debates. The logic of which approach to use would have to be determined by leadership and their perception of risk and reward of each option.

The process of developing the strategic plan as outlined in alternative 1 would be the same, with the exception of creating the marketing and lobbying approach prior to finalizing the strategic plan. System and university leadership would need to meet on a number of occasions to build a lobbying strategy centered on the maximum use of all internal constituencies. The identification of all participating constituencies and educating their leaders on the timing, substance, and desired outcomes of lobbying would take some lead time.

When the plan is approved by the board, it would be the first time to lay out the conditions of higher education relative to the reductions contemplated by the governor. The request would offer responses to the governor's demands on faculty and staff reductions, economic development connections, student tuition and fee options, and flexibility expectations, while simultaneously offering the dire circumstances if they were enacted.

The response from higher education would reflect the implications of loss in personal terms. The public would lose important programs supporting small businesses, agricultural programs, and vocational programs, and students would assume greater debt. Many communities would lose revenues as faculty and staff are terminated; quality may be impacted, which would drive lower public confidence and students will not be able to graduate in a timely fashion. State expectations for filling employment openings would have to be lowered and higher education would be unable to support many state-level priorities.

At the same time the governor and the public are assessing the implications of the executive request the strategic plan would offer ways to avoid or offset the cuts. The plan would offer areas for greater efficiencies, identify other fund sources, and also shift pressure to the state and argue for additional funds from the state to achieve the goals that benefit the state and its citizens. The submission would highlight the value of higher education to state residents in easily understood terms and emphasize the losses in practical and personal terms.

As the plan is circulated through various forums in the state and in conjunction with discussions with the governor and legislature, lobbying efforts would occur with internal and external constituencies. The degree of lobbying would be continuous through points of decision-making by the governor and the executive budget and then with the legislature until the appropriation is finalized.

Alternative 2 runs the real risk of failure if the resistance of the governor to higher education's lobbying is underestimated. The strategic plan addresses the points mandated by the governor; however, if they become secondary to the demands and protests of higher education constituencies, then the governor may hold fast or even suggest deeper losses.

If higher education leaders determine early in the development of the strategic planning process that they will move aggressively in opposition to the governor's recommendations, then they must identify conditions, specific to both positive and negative reactions, that will alter their strategy.

Conditions to alter higher education's approach to the governor's mandate:

- If higher education leaders see they may lose more than they gain once the lobbying has begun, how will they work to end any strife or destructive interactions? What are the signals to send, and when is the right time to offer a revised offer for consideration?
- Is there a point during the lobbying that both sides can sit down and gain a compromise that would allow both to move forward and neither "loses"? What suggests from the governor's public or private position that there is willingness for a compromise?
- If the governor takes a position that offers no hope for a compromise, how then does higher education limit losses? Can working with friendly legislators to get some relief? It is risky to seek relief from the legislature when the governor is adamant and active in arguing against higher education lobbying efforts. If legislative leadership is supportive, then some risk may be worthwhile.
- If higher education leaders offer a new proposal to shift attention away from what wasn't acceptable by moving closer to the governor's agenda, then some goodwill might be realized. When is the timing for introducing such a proposal right?

It is clear that modifying alternatives specific to given conditions is important for all leaders. While there may be a decision to support broadly conceived directions as suggested in alternatives 1 and 2, specific conditions based on immediate reactions of the governor and other internal and external constituencies should be considered.

The use of strategic planning and the planning and assessment framework helps formalize a wide array of options, even those that would alter existing agreements on timing and substance. That is, if a decision is made to follow alternative 2 in this scenario, then a corresponding list of related options should be developed that respond to the reactions of constituencies. The reactions create a new set of more current conditions that may alter the manner and substance in which leaders decide to communicate with the governor and other constituencies.

The conditions listed above relate to how the governor might respond to higher education's aggressive lobbying and create a need for leaders to rethink and modify their approach to having their programs funded. In this instance, the focus is on the governor's reactions, yet each constituency, internal and external, may not be completely onboard with modified options. It is critical for leadership to be certain sufficient strategic thinking and planning has gone into modifying proposals and that communications of those changes have been coordinated with appropriate constituency leaders.

Leaders should never be surprised by the reactions of constituencies to their choices!

CHAPTER 10

Internal Influences on Decisions (Cross-Cutting Issues)

IN THIS CHAPTER, we shift from a focus on a constituency-based analysis to specific issues that have differing values based on constituent priorities within an institution. The objective is to highlight the meaning and intensity of a given position within the context of constituent support or interest. We will be looking at issues from an internal perspective including students, faculty, institutional leaders, and system leadership. It will not consider external influences from leaders and constituencies outside of higher education like the governor's office, legislators, the public, etc. While there are countless issues of significance faculty compensation, tuition and fees and accountability will be examined. The interaction of key constituencies will be done by issue and not in summary per prior chapters. There will be an assessment of one of the issues, accountability, through the SDMM/planning and assessment framework.

Issues

Faculty Compensation

The salary and compensation of all employees in the operating budget of an institution represents the majority of all costs. The faculty salaries often represent the greatest share of all employee salaries. As funding declines, the faculty will be a logical target for scrutiny and cuts.

If the issue of faculty compensation was fully reviewed through the planning and assessment framework, the problem would be that as state funds are being reduced, it creates the secondary problem of how all institutional programs would be prioritized including faculty compensation. Faculty positions generally would be evaluated based on program priorities and their value in achieving the primary goals of the institution. The outcome would be that specific programs not achieving the goals of the department or institution would be reduced or eliminated and in turn faculty would be terminated.

The side effect of any short- or long-term loss of funds is that compensation increases are the first commitments to be put on hold. The theory that it is better to retain faculty and staff as opposed to increasing salaries has been a generally accepted standard. However, as reductions have become more chronic the option of not retaining the most productive faculty through compensation increases has become a real consideration. The loss of key faculty has repercussions in both teaching and the attraction of external grants to fund research initiatives. An institutional reputation depends in part on the productivity of faculty in instruction, research and service to the community and state.

The origin of faculty compensation issues has been with higher education for decades. However, as funding has declined there has been more attention paid to retention and compensation levels. The attention focused on how much a faculty member earned based on class workload. The public did not understand all the components of research, service, teaching and counseling that comprised a faculty member's workload. The outcome was a concern with the amount of compensation a faculty member made was based on the perception of a limited workload. The public perception made it easier to limit compensation increases for faculty. Ultimately, institutions had to make choices on giving retention funds to the most productive faculty while not giving increases to others.

How well faculty is compensated can have an impact on a number of constituencies. Students would hope to have the best faculty and enough of them to teach courses to get them through their degree in a timely fashion. Academic leaders want to retain and attract the best faculty but also acknowledging a fine balance between the quality and quantity of faculty. Institutional leaders would expect the reputation of their faculty to be competitive with peer institutions.

One alternative in addressing faculty compensation would be creating comparative institutional peer salary and benefits schedules by rank and discipline that would offer compensation benchmarks to help guide leaders in assessing need. If the institution's is below peer institutions generally by rank, then a plan could be established that justified a series of increases over time. While the politics of increases are not resolved by the alternative, it does give a rational standard that would be difficult to refute.

Tuition and Fees

Tuition and fees have become the primary resource for operating budget support in many public higher education systems and institutions. The funding for higher education was predominantly from state sources prior to the 1980s (approximately). The shift in funding has arisen from drops in state tax revenues and reallocated dollars for statewide health programs, growing correctional costs, and other programs with federal or state mandates. Public higher education and secondary education in most states did not benefit from legal mandates and were continuing sources for funding reductions.

The shift toward increased use of tuition and fees has been as an outcome of intentional and unintentional state decisions. The ideological desire to create smaller state governments has led to the intention of lowering tax rates and realizing fewer state revenues. The

2008 great recession was driven by the unintended consequence of reduced state revenues as derived from the shortsighted and faulty management of the economy at the federal level.

In any analysis of tuition and fees through the focus of the planning and assessment framework would be the intersection of intended and unintended consequences of lowered state revenues as the underlying problem. The commitment to public higher education diminished because it wasn't a legal mandate, and revenues continued to decline and because governors and legislators realized that other fund sources (e.g., tuition and fees) were available to support programs.

The origin of the problem began long before the great recession and a gradual drop in support in many states and gradual increases in tuition and fees. The seeds of public higher education becoming less and less a public good were in full bloom in the late '90s and up to the great recession when all bets were off for most state funded programs.

The constituency most affected by the declining state commitment is students. They continue to pay more money and, on any relative standard to the past, are receiving less in return. They may receive more technology, better labs, and even better resident halls, but they are paying a premium. The public is feeling the loss of a public good and each parent now has to be more concerned about the ability of their son or daughter to even attend a college or university. A portion of the public supports the notion that students pay full price for the higher education and thereby limit their tax bill. Faculty members feel the effects of downsizing through the reduction in academic programs, loss of faculty colleagues, and limited salary and compensation increases. There are honest efforts by faculty to readapt to a changing environment but with little sense that the program realignments and downsizing will not continue.

Alternatives for student tuition and fees center on finding some agreeable understanding of their "share" of funding in a state supported public higher education system. There has to be a red line for state officials to say they will not reduce higher education funding below a specified floor. If there is no such agreement, then the likely end is that funding will gradually degrade to a symbolic level of support and public higher education will have transitioned into private higher education. While it often seems that leaders do not appreciate the funding they receive from the state it is true any funding will help. However, as states reduce commitments by high single-digit and double-digit amounts, then the capacity for appreciation goes down as well.

Accountability

The third issue of accountability will be more fully explored through the planning and assessment framework.

Using the SDMM: Applying the Planning and Assessment Framework

Scenario—Accountability

An institution is in the midst its annual review of budget allocations. The revenues for the budget are 50% tuition and fees, 40% state funding, and 10% other fund sources. The state funding percentage has dropped by 10% over the last five years as the state commitment to higher education has diminished. Over the most recent years the institution has been creating accountability measures to better track success in attaining various objectives. The loss of state funds and increasing burden on the student has forced leaders to have better rationale in how funds are allocated and expended. Are programs getting the greatest "bang for the buck"? There is significant competition for dwindling resources among all constituencies and the logic used to allocate funds is more important than ever.

Higher Education Response

Institutional leadership must make decisions that respond to faculty demands for equitable salary allocations, technologically upgraded classrooms, and updated research facilities. Student demands must also be considered including enhanced resources to improve the learning experience through reasonable student faculty ratios, increased capacity to lower time to degree, more high-quality technology labs, updated living spaces, and attendance costs that allow for access for low-income and middle-income residents. Academic and administrative staff must be given the resources and facilities to do their jobs in support of instructional programming. All constituencies rely on a well-run institution whether it is an accurate and timely payroll, strong data system, clear academic and administrative policies for action, comprehensive student counseling and health services, proactive facilities department, vigilant campus safety department, and much more.

The demand for funding is growing among constituencies and requires academic and administrative leaders to create more and better measures of program performance. Over the years, there have been key performance indicators (KPIs), accountability measures, financial ratios, comparative changes in inputs and outputs, and outcomes that have been used to assess how programs have changed. The measures have not often been aligned with funding.

In its simplest form comparisons of growth or decline over one or more years were used to determine funding allocations. If enrollments grew by 5%, then an allocation x additional (increment) dollars would be added. Formulas, a representation of multiple objective data points, were and still are used to suggest a relationship between the data and financial need. They have been used in some form for over sixty years (Miller 1964). As funding declined over the years the cry for more refined analyses was sought to move beyond simplistic input and output data and formulas. The simple growth in enrollments wasn't sufficient enough by itself to justify an allocation of funding. A formula used to determine financial need for programs or institutions did not adequately incorporate key performance measures or outcomes. It should be noted that in many states where formulas were used to request funding they were specifically kept in simple combinations of variables to avoid a complexity that was confusing and could be self-defeating.

Hearn (2013), in his review of outcome-based funding in a paper to the Lumina Foundation, found that accountability measures have been seen as the most recent tool to attempt to measure performance and where possible, to build funding connections. In the very largest sense, the goal is to ensure that institutions are identifying their most important tasks and estimating how those tasks should increase over time, determine their value in dollars, and assess the change on a periodic basis. As the task changes, and there are increases or decreases, then so should the funding supporting the specific programs.

In this scenario, the institution is requiring that each administrative and academic unit identify five indicators and measures that best reflect the goals of their unit. Unit and institutional leaders would thoroughly debate the substance and value of the measures and eventually choose those that best represented the goals of instruction, research/discovery, public service, student services and support, facilities administration, and campus and public safety.

Planning and Assessment Framework

1. What is the problem? What creates instability? Is there agreement on the problem?

The overriding problem is determining how best to assess performance of programs and be certain that funding allocations are going to those that are most "deserving." All constituencies agree that the current means of assessing performance was a problem and felt their programs could benefit from a new way of allocating funds. There was no one group or constituency that felt the process of creating accountability measures was a major problem at the outset. In time the concern for the accountability measures had more to do with how the measures and related targets to determine success would affect the allocation of resources.

Instability arises from the perception and fact that budget allocations were not equitable. Also, any new method would create more competition for scarce resources with the only guarantee that there would be winners and losers. The possibility of losing funding created instability and eventually became an issue as the processes unfolded.

2. What examples contribute to the problem? What is the magnitude of the problem?

The problem felt by all constituencies was that current methods of allocating resources were not necessarily equitable. Budget allocations had been made for additional funding to programs that did not necessarily grow in quantity or quality. There had been historical base increases provided to academic programs that were no longer growing or meeting prior year's goals. The institution must establish a plan that recognizes priorities and desired outcomes to avoid continuing funding allocations that no longer meet current demands.

In this instance, the institution will redefine the accountability measures that will be most representative in meeting the institutional goals. Each unit has the opportunity to justify its funding expectations through the acceptance of their goals, programs, and related measures.

The severity of the problem will be clear when the final decisions are made on which program measures are used to fund the most important programs. Many programs may see allocations drop if they ae viewed as less valued while others will be increased and given a higher value. Of course, over time even those that benefit the most will have to perform to standards that may not always to be achieved.

The original problem of the perception of inequitable distribution of funds will be replaced with the concern that the new methodology of allocating funds may not be as equitable as hoped (at least by those who felt they should have received a greater share of funding).

3. What is the origin of the current examples of the problem? What caused the problem?

The origin of the problem is the continuing decline in resources and need to allocate funds in the most efficient and effective way possible. One could go back and see at various junctures in time that different means of allocating resources were used based on then current thought and practice. Formulas came about in the '60s in response to a more objective perspective in making funding decisions. Many of the formulas were created at the state level to allocate funds across systems of higher education. The allocations to institutions were made based on how the numbers in the formulas treated each institution. Even though an institution did not have to develop internal budgets based on the statewide formula, they still received an appropriation based on the "fit" with various factors. Factors included the growth or decline in measurable variables such faculty, staff, institutional square footage, counseling visits, campus safety workloads, etc.

Formulas continue today in some states while in others there is a focus on outcomes and other accountability measures. In this scenario, outcome measures are the "new" means of connecting performance with funding. It is assumed the concerns with equity will be reduced with the connection of funding to performance.

4. Is there a historical precedent for the problem? Does the precedent connect with current issues?

In recent years, it has been seen that many states are looking at the use of different budget methodologies as they deal with fewer and fewer state funds. As suggested formulas originated as a means to link key higher education variables like enrollments, historical expenditure growth, number of faculty and staff, etc., to discrete funding requirements. The era of the seventies found the federal government using Planned Program Budgeting System (PPBS). PPBS was a tool to project funding need based on program goals and numerous data points used to measure program quantity and quality.

Today connecting accountability to funding is as important as ever. The accountability measures now used are more refined and the ability to capture and assess data is more sophisticated. The ability to look more deeply into programs, colleges, departments, and disciplines, as well as multiple categories of students such as being resident or nonresident, being international, ethnicity, religion, color, major, and other information, is well beyond what was done even a decade ago. Ideally institutions have been aware of the strategies of using accountability measures and can adapt their data system and reporting efforts to react quickly to funding shifts that have been occurring for at least twelve years.

5. Which constituencies are most affected? Do all constituencies feel there is a problem? What is the relative stake for each?

All faculty and staff are affected by a movement toward new allocation methodologies. Students have relatively no stake in the process to change performance measurement and funding allocations. Not all constituencies feel there is a problem because they are content with their budget. From their perspective why change a process that works.

Each constituency must identify their most important programs and the means of measuring their success. What they can measure is a reflection of who they are and becomes the point of comparison with other institutional programs. It is the comparison across all other units and institutional goals that foster's competition and uncertainty. Once there are decisions on specific accountability measures, there still may not be an acceptance by all constituencies. As mentioned earlier there are always winners and losers in the competition for resources. How constituencies and related programs compete in attracting more or less resources will affect their view on the equity of the process for years to come.

If there are enough constituencies that feel the process was lacking in its capacity to capture all appropriate facets of their work, they will seek an alternative or at least some recognition and guarantee for future support.

6. Provide alternatives or actions on how to strategically prepare for and address similar examples in the future.

A number of alternatives could be considered regarding the type, use and timing of development and implementation of accountability measures. This alternative will focus on one comprehensive approach. At a minimum one alternative should focus on the process of how to coordinate the development of accountability measures with maximum input from each constituency. The comprehensive nature of the process should limit any fallout from lack of transparency and outcomes chosen. While accountability measures by themselves don't require a full-blown use of the SDMM, each of the components will have varying roles in the success of the process. Strategic thinking will be essential, transparency and communications key variables, utilizing a strategic planning methodology with some attention to future scanning and global awareness is critical and as we will see in this example the planning and assessment framework indispensable.

In advance of developing our alternative, let's summarize the conditions confronted by public higher education as posed by the board. Below are the assumptions:

- New methods of allocating funds within an institution are necessary.
- The necessity for change is driven by reduced funding and the related growing competition among program priorities.
- The funding from the state has dropped from 50% of the operating budget to 40% while student tuition and fees has risen to 50%.
- The institutional leadership is creating a process to reset allocation strategies with a focus on accountability measures.
- All constituencies will be asked to develop at least five accountability measures that can be assessed against the primary goals and priorities of the institution.

- The process will generate accountability measures that will be used to determine funding allocations and as a basis for discussions both internally and externally.

Alternative

Changing how an institution funds its programs is among the most difficult challenges in higher education. The problems inherent with change are many:

- Gaining buy-in from constituencies from the outset and throughout a process
- Fearing potential loss of funding by all constituencies
- Having enough data to make decisions
- Having data that all can agree on
- Agreeing on the major institutional goals and priorities
- Choosing participants for the process
- Timing of the process
- Implication of negative outcomes on budgets
- Rallying internal and external constituencies to influence the process
- Having a process that is transparent
- Competing with other institutional units

Any planning process that is being considered must identify all collateral problems and deal with them before the process begins. The SDMM includes a comprehensive strategic planning process that addresses potential problems from the beginning. Leadership must be capable of responding to constituent questions before they are asked. The model component of strategic thinking requires an awareness of current positions, processes, and goals as future changes are being considered. The allocation of funding is the key indication of the value place on the goals and strategies as represented in the system and institutional budgets. Ultimately, the institutional budgets provide the capacity, however limited, for leaders to identify priorities and where possible measure success.

Participation in a process that is redefining budget allocations should be well represented by all constituencies and transparent to all. When the process is concluded, there should be no one who can say that there weren't forums for debate on what measures were important and why, relative to each constituency. Students should be able to offer thoughts on measures they feel are important in decision-making. They continue to absorb increasing costs and deserve attention. They may feel that the institution should put greater weight on finding fund sources outside of tuition and fees.

The proposal might highlight accountability measures that reflected incentives for funding from federal grants/overhead, incubator programs, fund-raising activities, and other entrepreneurial efforts. The institution that could grow other sources would be given an incentive but also be able to reduce tuition and fee supported budgets with the new revenues.

Students may also want to limit future tuition and fees through the use of peer comparisons. Each institution may have multiple peers that are similar in mission, size, budget, research category, urban/rural, etc. Measures of average tuition and fees could be developed that set ceilings and floors on tuition such that institutions could not increase tuition beyond the ceiling (or some other limit). Even if the institution didn't want to limit its flexibility in setting tuition, it would open up the debate as to what is fair to the student and how that should factor into overall decision-making.

Faculty measures have grown over the years from student enrollments by class, course, discipline, and college; to student faculty ratios; to quality of programs based on accreditation by discipline, faculty research, and scholarship outputs. Faculty would be seeking to maximize their visibility in the overall process and put the value of their programs front and center. The more-typical outcomes such as time to degree awarded, student faculty ratios, faculty research, and public service would be considered. There are more subjective measures such as evaluations by students, academic leaders, and peers that could be considered.

Institutional and system leaders are presented an opportunity to identify continuing program strengths and redefining areas of lower priority in this scenario. Whatever choices they make will have impacts on all constituencies and the organizational structure as a whole. If through the strategic planning process, they build alternatives that will shift resources from programs that are no longer of high priority, then they will feel the frustrations of the advocates for the programs being diminished. They will have to face faculty, students, program leaders, and even the public in justifying the changes that are being considered. It is through the planning processes that the first signs of program expansion and downsizing should be discussed. That is, if the priority is to move more actively in hard sciences as opposed to other program areas, then that should have been raised early to gain as much input as possible. The SDMM offers the vehicle through which leaders can expose all ideas, gauge their relative value, and set a course.

Any discussion of shifting of resources from one or more programs must include how other programs will benefit. Any communications efforts must highlight how the institution will be stronger with a focus on the hard sciences and better able to meet the program and demographic needs as highlighted throughout the strategic planning and assessment processes.

In this instance, the creation of accountability measures is developed, focusing on a new set of program priorities (along with other continuing programs and services), and funding allocations will be built from those measures. While there will be winners and losers relative to prior years, it is critical for leaders to place a strong emphasis on the values gained moving into the future. If the programs and services are not realigned, the institution will not be successful.

The full use of the six components of the SDMM in identifying the programs that would be of lower and higher priority and the related organizational and funding implications would be critical. Positive outcomes could be realized through active, thoughtful, and comprehensive strategic planning and assessment; a focus on better understanding what the future holds; in-depth, information-based research planning; and full transparency to all internal and external constituencies.

CHAPTER 11

External Influences on Internal Decisions

In this chapter, attention will be on issues that affect public higher education as generated from external constituencies. While there are issues, mandates, and events that originate outside of the decision-making purview of higher education they have very real implications for the internal constituencies of higher education. It is useful to understand at least some of the issues that can have an impact on internal decision-making. It is incumbent on leaders to recognize how their strategic decisions can be altered, for better or worse, by external authorities. The use of the SDMM and planning and assessment framework in identifying the sources of external actors and the form and magnitude of their influence is critical in the overall decision-making.

The external sources of influence include the governor's office, governor's offices of policy, budgeting, finance and planning oversight, the legislature, attorney general, state auditor, accrediting agencies, federal agencies, local community agencies, state highway department, and local and state police residing in each campus community.

The governor's office is the most influential in funding programs, setting priorities for the state broadly, establishing guidelines for agency strategic planning and budgeting, ensuring policies are followed, and seeking input on issues that are of particular interest to the public. The influence is further seen in the ability to make appointments to boards of higher education in many states.

The offices dealing with planning, budgeting, finance, and policy are sometimes directly connected with the governor's office and other times separate. Each has an important function meeting the goals of the governor. The planning office oversees program planning for all state agencies and offers analyses on higher education goals and strategic connection with the state. The budget office leads on a review of the state budget with attention to how well higher education has addressed statewide goals, funding guidelines, and accountability measures. The finance division assesses the use of state funds to ensure that all administrative and legislative requirements are met. The policy office would also review higher education strategic plans and other board policies on human resources, public safety, campus gun policies, etc., to determine their connection to corresponding state policies. Different states have different organizational structures to accomplish oversight responsibilities, but they would generally follow the aforementioned planning, budget, finance, and policy functions.

Other state organizations have specific roles, like the attorney general and state auditor. They act as legal resources in ensuring that state and federal laws are followed, and that legislative intent is enforced. Higher education, through the system and at each institution, is subject to oversight of both of these very important functions.

Issues

Accreditation by Discipline and Institution

Every institution that award a degree to a student must have an accreditation by a regional accreditation body. If the degree awarded is not from an accredited institution, its value in the marketplace is zero. The student will be unable to use the degree as a resource in gaining employment or showing some level of proficiency in their field of study.

Accreditation means that an external authority can evaluate academic programs and make judgments regarding ability to meet acceptable standards of quality and resource support. Individual programs or disciplines are assessed as are entire institutions.

Financial Aid—Federal and State Aid

State and federal financial aid programs often work independently of institutions in making decisions on the amount of funds awarded to students. The grants or aid eventually become part of the institution's financial resources but only as a pass through to students. The amounts awarded are most frequently awarded based on economic need. The institution can supplement need based funds with scholarship- or merit-based funds depending on the guidelines of a particular program and the qualifications of the student.

The policies of federal and state financial aid offices are extremely important in defining how much funding a student receives, when it will be received, and ongoing follow-up in issues related to eligibility and dispute resolution.

State Economic Development Policies

Many states have economic development offices that are charged to increase the economic vitality of the state. They are able to create partnerships with all local and state communities in identifying initiatives that benefit the community and the state. In many instances they are seen as the catalysts in bringing about job creation through those relationships. Needless to say, if a governor can say jobs are being created through such programs under executive auspices it is of great practical and political value. Higher education is often asked to submit initiatives that could benefit their local community and participate in broader statewide proposals that stress multiple partners (e.g., multiple higher education institutions with one another or other state agencies in achieving common objectives).

State Planning and Budget Mandates

The issues surrounding the state role in planning and budgeting will be discussed through the planning and assessment framework.

Using the SDMM: Applying the Planning and Assessment Framework

Scenario

External influences on higher education come in many forms. There may be direct mandates from the governor or legislature, audit findings on institutional programs, accreditation recommendations, legal opinions and directives, federal funding reductions, and much more.

In this scenario, we will be reviewing the implications of a state planning and budget office on higher education. The office receives its oversight from the governor but has substantial latitude as the statewide function dealing with planning and budgeting. It requests periodic strategic plans from every agency including the state system of higher education and each individual institution. It assesses the progress on meeting the approved plans annually and offers comments and recommendations that are shared with the governor's office. The recommendations are viewed as serious inputs regarding process and substance. It also coordinates the annual budget development processes and review of budget requests. It may also seek multi-year budget plans paralleling the strategic plans as means of gauging the consistency in program and funding requests.

A state planning and budgeting office made the following requests of all state agencies:

- Develop a five-year strategic plan built on vision, mission, and goals of the system of higher education and each institution.
- Include in the plan the specific programs necessary to achieve the mission and goals.
- Include in the plan outcome measures necessary to measure success.
- Reflect the projected progress in outcome measures over the five-year period.
- Detail funding needs for each program annually over the five-year period.
- Connect the funding required with outcome measures over the five-year period.
- Include in the plan initiatives that will support statewide goals in economic development.
- Identify the five primary priorities of the institution and how they will be achieved.
- Identify potential funding reallocations to achieve success without new state funding.

Higher Education Response

The chancellor took the planning and budget office charge and met with the board to discuss the strategies that would be necessary to be successful in the process and outcomes of the planning mandate. The board approved a timeline, points of communication, and general planning goals. The chancellor shared the board's input and developed a strategy for moving forward with the institutional presidents.

Broadly speaking the primary reaction to the request was first making assumptions how the information would be used by the state office. If the intention was to reduce funding, then it would be necessary that all submissions were fair and accurate but also of high advocacy for the programs.

Second, it would be important to create a response that was consistent with system goals and outcome measures, while being consistent across all institutions. The avoidance of any outlying differences, within reason of varying missions, would be important in maintaining a unified front.

Third, the alignment of budget with outcome measures had to be thoughtful and capable of scrutiny over time. There would be little value in projecting increases in various outcome measures to gain some immediate budget increase. In fact, if the measures did not reach targeted levels, then there would be even greater concern for the funding allocated and voracity of the process. There are many who would look for outcome targets that aren't achieved so they can project failure to the entire request. The budget requests must be as real in the second, third, fourth, and fifth years as it is in the first.

All constituencies should be actively engaged in any process that defines outcome measures. Students, faculty, academic leaders, institutional leaders, and others representing specific programs need to have a voice. The current budgets represent the starting point for any funding debate for internal and external constituencies. The capacity to add to or subtract from that base budgets when considering the implications of outcome measures is critical. The strength of the request will be on how honest it is perceived to be in both program offerings and funding projections.

Planning and Assessment Framework

1. What is the problem? What creates instability? Is there
   agreement on the problem?

The problem is twofold. One problem is the development of a planning and budgeting request that may be seen as a vehicle to reduce budgets. On the surface the request by the planning and budget office makes sense. However, in an era of budget reductions the call for connecting planning, budgeting and outcome measures has the potential to be used as a tool for further reductions.

A second problem is the potential for increased competition among the internal constituencies to benefit from any added funds or alternatively, and more negatively, to compete to avoid any further reductions.

The first problem is driven by external demands which ultimately creates the internal concern

The request has mixed reactions and does not at the outset create any instability. Not all constituencies see the request as threatening. The hope is that the products of the process will be used to grow advocacy for higher education. Others feel that information provided to the planning and budget office will be used to downsize public higher education in future budget cycles.

2. What examples contribute to the problem? What is the
   magnitude of the problem?

The problem will become more manifest when there is belief that the products of the process will be misused. Thus, it is important from the outset to build rationale that highlights what will occur if they are not adequately funded. What are the implications for the institutions if they have to cut faculty, raise tuition, limit student enrollments, and do other downsizing measures? There is a merging of the two problems identified in the first question. The external demand for more detailed information is viewed more realistically as threatening to the institutions. The processes, then used to respond to the planning and budget office, while complying with the request, will provide more defensive support as to the implications for the public if there are further cutbacks.

The severity of the problem grows as there an assumption that the processes, and products will be used as tools for loss as opposed to gain.

3. What is the origin of the current examples of the problem? What
   caused the problem?

The planning and budget office has periodically requested multiyear strategic planning information. The request is made of all state agencies. In prior years, there have been occasions when the information has been used to reduce budgets and other instances where they have supported increased funding. In the years of decline, the system was given the flexibility to target the cuts in the programs identified by each institution.

4. Is there a historical precedent for the problem? Does the precedent connect with current issues?

There is historical precedence that does connect with current tissues. Leaders have the opportunity to look at the use of the planning information in prior years and determine the circumstances that have led to examples when the budget office has made reductions. In those years when budgets were reduced the conditions of the state were such that revenues supporting state agencies had declined over prior years.

In this planning process it is assumed that a budget may be cut or increased based on the success in achieving performance goals. Thus, if a program is not successful they could be cut regardless of the state funding situation. Also, it might be inferred that budgets can be reduced if the state has revenue shortfalls even if it does achieve its pre-determined goals.

The state then has an opportunity, connected to performance, to either add or subtract funds based on measurable outcomes and reduce funds when state revenues don't meet projected estimates.

5. Which constituencies are most affected? Do all constituencies feel there is a problem? What is the relative stake for each?

All constituencies must be willing to actively engage in the institution wide strategic planning processes. It seems likely that the budget and planning office will use the reports along with their analyses to inform the governor on key issues. It may be the plans will eventually be used for downsizing higher education or may be used to determine where increases should be allocated. In either case, student leaders, faculty senates, system leaders, and institutional leaders must place a high priority on completing the process. At a minimum they should be able to create findings and recommendations that can be used for marketing higher education programs. The public will be interested in the benefits of a higher education and why reductions will be detrimental to all state citizens.

Students don't recognize the importance of the process and many faculties are unaware of the potential implications on their programs. As an outcome, neither feels they have as much at stake in the process and pay less attention to their respective leaders. It is assumed that the deeper the institution is in the strategic planning process in identifying outcomes and relative funding targets, the greater their interest will be. The stakes will be relatively higher for all as there is more clarity regarding the use of the information.

6. Provide alternatives or actions on how to strategically prepare for and address similar examples in the future.

The primary alternative under consideration is one that works to fully comply with the planning and budget office as requested. The alternative will also feature additional observations and recommendations that go beyond the requested outline as a means to accurately portray the goals, objectives, priorities, outcomes, etc., at a more finite level.

The board could consider a second alternative and take the stance that any submission where the primary motive is to cut budgets would provide justification for a more aggressive and perhaps less specific and robust response.

In this instance, higher education will take the request and build on it. In advance of developing the alternative, let's summarize the conditions confronted by public higher education as posed by the planning and budget office of the state. They are as follows:

- Develop system and institutional five-year strategic plans including vision, mission, goals, and outcome measures.
- Identify the programs necessary to achieve the mission and goals.

- Provide projections for outcome measures over a five-year period.
- Provide funding requirements for all programs over a five-year program.
- Connect funding and outcome measures over the same five-year period.
- Include initiatives that will support statewide economic development goals.
- Identify the five primary priorities of each institution and how they will be achieved.
- Identify potential funding reallocations to achieve success without new state funding.

The requirements are comprehensive and time consuming in thought and action. The scenario laid out the actions taken by the chancellor in conjunction with the board and institutional leaders. As should be the case in all exercises that share information with external constituencies, it is necessary for the system and institutions to be on the same page in terms of substance, timing, process, marketing and lobbying strategies, and desired outcomes. If there are any presidents that move in directions that put other institutions or the system at some risk, then actions must be taken to stop or limit the damage. The earliest stages of the strategic planning process should be focused on identifying how institutions might differ and how those differences should be acknowledged. If there is an active discussion and debate on differences in planning and budget outcomes, they should be set as the strategic planning committee begins its work.

The SDMM represents the text book application in addressing this particular scenario. There must be substantial thought on existing mission, goals, funding requirements, program data, enrollment projections, outcome measures, and much more in the earliest stages of the strategic planning process. It is important to understand current planning expectations, environmental conditions and real commitments before any new strategies are developed.

In this alternative, it is paramount that communications between constituencies is frequent and comprehensive. From the development of the agreements of how to approach the entire process (i.e., the what, who, how, and when of the strategic planning process) to the point of submitting the report to the planning and budget office, active communication is paramount. The wide-ranging involvement of students, faculty, staff, leaders, board members, external representatives, etc., demands a heightened communications strategy. Transparency is a necessary component as outlined in the SDMM. The principles of transparency of process, participation, timing, and actions give meaning to the necessity of communicating all aspects of the strategic planning process. It is the goal of the chancellor to follow those principles to ensure all constituents have opportunities to offer suggestions, debate potential strategies, and provide feedback on eventual decisions.

From a strategic standpoint, the decision was made to offer more information and analyses in the response than requested by the planning and budget office. The goal was to offer a more sophisticated assessment of future opportunities and potential risks. They took the five-year time horizon and lengthened it to eight years. The intention was to be able to highlight how progress might take place in a longer time frame (assuming that if it appears too limited in five years the eight-year cycle might be more accurate). Similarly, if decline or only limited growth was seen over five years, then the eight-year cycle would be a better representation.

In areas where budgets were linked to outcomes over a five- or eight-year-period care was taken in highlighting how specific events or conditions could change the projections. In each case, a key variable was the projection of state funding. If state funding did not reach levels projected, then the outcome measures would also be unable to reach targets. The simple point being that, if the state didn't meet its funding commitments, then higher education outcome measures would not reach their levels. That is, enrollments may not reach estimated levels without added state funding, or economic development initiatives may not be undertaken without state support, or student time to graduation may not improve without sufficient state monies; and on.

Each institution and the system identified ten priorities they felt were critical in meeting the goals of the future. It was felt that by only offering the requested five priorities, there would be a very shortsighted and restrictive view of what higher education institutions are facing. In effect by only providing five it would give the incorrect impression that if reductions were being considered then anything not listed would be too easily discounted.

The system-level committee offered ten priorities of the board from a statewide perspective. Each institutional committee used those in building their own list but with expectations that there would be some variations. If the system supported enrollment growth broadly, there may be one institution that did not expect to grow based on conditions of mission, size, programming location, etc., and as such would not include that in its list of ten. The board could support expanding the number of campuses to a new city. Each institution wouldn't have to include that item unless they might want to offer suggestions on how they can support the initiative.

Each campus might have a unique priority to include in their submission. The unique priority should be summarized in the system plan, a plan that can be a valuable resource that highlights and embraces differences where they make sense with the programming of a given institution. As an example, a community college offering a vocational program that is unique to their location and population and differing from system priorities is not unusual. It may even be that the system priorities could be revised to give general acknowledgment to the differences and get credit for recognizing that one size does not fit all.

The planning and budget office request for how institutions would use reallocated funds (i.e., funds that are already in a budget that can be moved to address another purpose) should be considered with great concern. While the intent may simply be to reinforce how the highest priorities would be funded using existing funds, it presents a trap. The trap is that if an institution identifies that it will take $1 million from administrative support programs and put it into enrollment and recruitment efforts, then there are irreparable consequences for the administrative programs. The outside analyst can assume that the administrative programs are able to sustain the loss under any circumstance and would see that as a target in the future. Similarly, if a community college decides to shift one hundred thousand dollars from a productive program to bolster one that isn't progressing as hoped, then the productive program may be viewed as target in future years. Success could be rewarded with a loss of funding.

It is important that all the strategic planning committees keep the consequences of their actions in mind. A finding, conclusion, or strategy that makes sense to a committee may have a very different meaning to an analyst working in the planning and budget office. Reviewing the implications and context of key findings and strategies is critical.

In this alternative, if the internal planning committees applied the components of the SDMM, they would be successful in providing responses to the planning and budget office that addresses state and higher education goals. Taking steps to provide more information than required and clarifying implications of reduced state funding would be strategically wise. The efforts by the chancellor to maximize transparency, offer greater participation by constituencies and thereby lessen chances that the process would be difficult to criticize later down the road.

The ultimate value of the system and institutional strategic planning efforts was to take the opportunity to redefine and realign programs over eighteen years and with the full participation of all constituencies. It was a resetting of system directions that could be used for years as a basis for decision-making at the system and institutional levels. The implications from the state perspective would be unknown until the planning and budget office presents their own report to the governor and the public. At a minimum, higher education presented information that would shed light on the implications of added funding and the risk in meeting statewide goals if funding was reduced.

CHAPTER 12

Application of the Strategic Decision-Making Model

THROUGHOUT THE BOOK the focus has been on identifying specific situations or scenarios where institutional leaders have had to react to demands from both internal and external constituencies. In chapter 3, there was a discussion of the concept of big-P politics as represented by formal political parties and little-p politics as represented by the interests of competing constituencies within higher education. Both were defined as political, with one external to higher education and the other a product from within higher education. In each case, the constituents had goals, program priorities and funding expectations that defined who they were and often put them in competition with other priorities and constituencies. It is the competition that drove various levels of cooperation and where there was conflict, compromise.

Many scenarios were discussed that "forced" constituencies to create plans that acknowledged the points of conflict with other parties. If a constituent group was to be successful, it had to isolate the strengths and weaknesses of their competitors (i.e., those seeking the same scarce resources they were). The essence of the competition was the degree to which each constituency was willing to build or break down relationships that would help them achieve their goals. If there is intense competition among multiple constituencies for scarce resources, then dissent would be magnified and cooperation and compromise less likely. Each alternative in each scenario provided "solutions" that offered different reactions and conclusions to the same scenario. The alternatives represented varying approaches that recognized political influences in the final decisions. The differences between alternatives were in how the external constituencies might react to higher education initiatives from a political big-P way. Higher education constituencies, those internal to the system and institutions, reacted to the governor and legislature, or external constituencies, based on the strategic plans and requests they had developed from the little-p political perspective. The degree to which there was cooperation and compromise was dependent on many factors including the intersection of goals, strategic objectives, funding availability versus expectations, historical agreements, and the depth of the external and internal investments in their own plans.

Constituent versus Constituent

There were a number of scenarios that assumed the state would be reducing funding and generally had done so for a number of years leading up to the recommendation. The typical response was to cut programs, raise student tuition, and limit any compensation commitments to the faculty and staff. As a consequence of consistent loss of state funds, the stage was set for competition among the constituencies for scarce resources. The most notable points of competition would be the students versus institutional leadership, faculty versus institutional leadership, and students versus faculty. (In addition to the faculty, staff, and leadership, there would be subsets of nonfaculty staff in student services, facilities, campus safety, and library, to name a few, that would be seeking considerations to respond to their more specific needs.) The competitions represented the political interactions of internal constituencies, or little-p politics. The institutional leadership would offer strategies supporting their recommendations while students and faculty would create counterarguments. If the students were unhappy with the responses, they would attempt to organize marches and forums to highlight their sense of disconnect from the administration. The tension could escalate to the extent that the students would lobby the governor and legislature to give clarity to their issues that weren't addressed in the higher education plans and budget. They would also seek other considerations to soften the leadership's recommendations including more student technology labs, reduced emphasis in the future on student tuition, demanding of other nonstudent sources of revenue, and other resources that support students beyond current levels. The students looked for some form of compromise. If they thought they couldn't change tuition rates, then they needed some other sign from the administration that they were valued.

On the faculty side, they would continue to demand increases in compensation but use the faculty senate as the bully pulpit. The faculty senate leaders would create forums for faculty dissent and like the students go to the public and legislature to create a statewide awareness of their treatment. Obviously the better their argument the more it could resonate with the public and in turn put pressure on leadership. Again they, like the students, could go beyond the system and pressure leaders to change the recommendations. The competition followed by limited cooperation may lead to dissent and potentially compromise (or greater conflict).

It should be noted in both the faculty and student examples they may lose bargaining power in the future if they appear to leaders and the public to be too aggressive in their approach. In times of extreme financial difficulty, it is not always easy to find sympathetic supporters for constituencies who are perceived as arguing against other constituencies or the institutions themselves. Thus, even if the students get a short-term benefit through compromise they may lose any long-term bargaining power. They will have sacrificed for immediate rewards but damaged the opportunities for students or faculty in the future.

There were a number of scenarios that had very positive relationships between internal constituencies built with a mutual understanding of addressing the attacks made by external constituencies.

The united front created a much more difficult barrier for legislators and the governor's office to dissect and divide. While it may have not benefited all parities equally in the final tally it would have reflected well on the system and institutional leader's capacity to coordinate and communicate a common message and recommendations that helped all parties.

Building Strategic Decisions by Using the SDMM

In prior chapters, we focused on scenarios that were assessed through the P and A framework. In this chapter, we will examine a scenario through each of the six components of the model. We will be looking at decisions made through active strategic thinking that benefits from a global analysis with future scanning features. A strategic planning process will be at the center of the process feeding the P and A framework information on goals, timing, process, findings, analytical assessments, outcomes, and outcome measures. The overall success depends on its transparency with all constituencies, internal and external.

The purpose of going beyond the application of the P and A framework is to highlight the necessity to integrate the six components into a thoughtful and interconnected assessment model, a model (SDMM) that offers the best opportunity for successful decision-making. While leaders are focused most on identifying and solving problems, any inattention to communications, transparency, future focus, implications of worldwide events, and very thoughtful strategic thinking (beyond the immediate problems), will render the decisions that are made of less value to many constituencies. In fact, the decisions that are made, no matter how strategic and timely, can be disputed before they are implemented. Disputes and limited support can arise from a lack of inclusivity of all constituencies, an ineffective communications strategy throughout the process, an inaccurate or limited scan of future events, a strategic planning approach that does not consider all relevant information, and simply underestimating the complexity of variables interacting within and without the higher education environment. In short, all six components are important in contributing to leadership decision-making.

Internal and External Politics—How to Compete, Cooperate, and Compromise

There are countless points of internal and external interactions that can be characterized by competition, cooperation, and compromise. The interactions can be particularly political internally if the components of the SDMM are not fully in play as suggested in the prior paragraph and constituencies feel they are not being dealt with fairly. The political unrest, when dealing externally with the public, governor's office, the legislature, federal government, etc., can be quite bitter. Bitterness can come from a sense of distrust in process and measures, lack of transparency on either side, misunderstanding of historical agreements, and other areas of overlap. External politics is an arena that is more difficult to navigate both upstream and downstream and is more often than not out of the control of higher education leaders.

A final scenario will be introduced that offers the variables from which higher education leaders must react and respond. It will demand a greater depth of analysis by leaders and constituencies. The implications of making choices not born out by the information or not following the basic tenets of the SDMM will have negative consequences to leaders and their constituencies.

As opposed to outlining multiple alternatives, there will be one alternative that will be viewed through each of the SDMM components. Pros and cons will be offered by component as the alternative is developed. The components of the SDMM are defined below:

- **Strategic thinking** by all constituencies is ongoing. It is a key component of the SDMM and should establish the foundation for strategic planning efforts from the point of initiation to the development of final strategies. Strategic thinking should continually consider the environment and the implications on system and institutional vision, mission, goals, outcomes, etc., and offer insights that guide leaders as they consider change.

- **Information, data, and analyses** are the bedrock of any meaningful strategic planning process. The number, timeliness, and quality of data and related analyses are what establish the credibility of the decisions. Bad information begets bad analyses begets bad decisions.
- **Future scans** give leaders and planners information that can guide thinking beyond current events, existing organizational structures, and historical visions and missions on a state, national, and international level. The future scan goes beyond many typical institutional approaches at looking into the future by creating continuing reviews and assessments of processes and events outside of higher education in social, economic, military, medical, and other areas. The analysis of what is happening outside of higher education nationally and globally may have a direct or indirect connection in the programs and services offered by higher education.
- **Strategic planning** is the primary vehicle in ensuring that all components of the SDMM are actively engaged. It covers all aspects from process, timing, communications strategies, forums for education and debate, input and feedback loops, leadership meetings with internal and external leaders, connection to the P and A framework, and source for all leadership decisions. It is the beginning and ending point of planning where final strategies are structured into plans that connect all constituencies.
- **Transparency** requires that all constituencies be aware of the planning processes taking place within an institution and have the opportunity for input, debate, and reaction to outcomes. The application of the principles of transparency that include process, participation, timing, and action ensures involvement of all constituencies. If planning processes are not transparent then students, faculty, external constituencies, and the public will be far less interested in

fighting for their implementation, particularly if they did not benefit from the decisions.

- The **planning and assessment framework** is the primary tool to raise the questions and assess the answers that help guide leaders in the strategic planning process. It gives leaders a structure to consistently apply against all problems. It does not make final decisions for leaders but provides the answers and analyses that help them as they create strategies and eventually formulate those strategies into an overall plan. If properly used with good data and analyses, it will identify contradictory positions, irrelevant historical priorities, "hidden" mandates, and new options for decision makers and generally create a vetting process that goes well beyond typical planning methodologies.

Each of the model's components will offer insights on how to best manage through the conditions of the scenario. That is, if an institution did not use a strategic planning process or there was limited transparency then those omissions or conditions would be highlighted. There would be a discussion of why the decision made by leaders would be marginalized because of lack of the absence of the two components and the probable inability to get support for the decisions from multiple constituencies. It is hoped that many of the shortcoming of leadership decisions will become self-evident and easily avoided.

In each component there will be reference to the politics of given situations. There is the possibility, even likelihood that external and internal, big-P and little-p politics respectively, will come into play. The presence of politics may be in process, timing, inclusivity, goal setting, funding requirements, external demands, perceptions, and realities that agitate constituencies into competition. Competition that leads to varying levels of cooperation and compromise based on each circumstance.

Scenario

The state has reduced higher education funding for four consecutive years based on continuing tax reductions and a willingness to see higher education support programs through greater tuition. The legislature had been controlled by one party for six years with the governor from a different party. Redistricting has created a new majority party and has opened up opportunities in the upcoming legislative session. The state senate majority and governor are now from the same party.

The governor has called for a no increase budget for higher education in the upcoming year with promises for future growth if tax revenues increase. The governor is seeking higher education support in the areas of economic development, resident access to higher education, formula funding for budget setting, and new outcome measures that indicate progress or success toward achieving key priorities. There is a specific requirement to growth student resident enrollment by 15% over the next three years.

The governor requests that the board of higher education give greater authority to each institution through delegation of personnel and facilities functions now residing with the board. Also, institutions are asked to provide plans that would identify administrative functions that could be consolidated with increased efficiency.

The legislature is introducing a bill to eliminate the state board and replace it with separate boards at every institution for a total of five new university boards and ten community college boards. Each institution would respond to the governor and legislature as individual units.

Students are beginning organizing efforts to lay out their case for no tuition increases and new funding for technology support. Faculty senates are lobbying leaders to develop a process that addresses compensation inequities relative to peers and demanding more say in their governance at the board level. If they can't attain some autonomy, then the idea of separate institutional boards appears more attractive, if not ideal.

There have been isolated discussions by other institutional advocates supporting the idea of disengaging from the state board and gaining autonomy, they feel will free them from the burdens of the board authority and oversight.

The state board has reacted strongly to the legislative recommendation that it be eliminated. It is beginning to provide to all internal and external constituents the preliminary negative impacts of decentralized policy and financial decisions spread out over fifteen different institutions. Through their immediate reactions they are making it clear to institutional leaders that they won't tolerate lobbying that supports the decentralization.

(There is an ironic juxtaposition of the intentions of the governor and legislature. The governor seeks statewide solutions through formula funding, outcome measure development and access for state residents. Even the decentralization of two administrative functions falls far short of termination of the system and board. Solutions will be most efficiently developed and monitored annually under a system or more centralized authority.

The legislative intent to decentralize will almost certainly get fifteen different formulas, outcome measures that are not tested against other institutions, and access (enrollment) modeling that isn't connected to statewide needs. As one example, the governor's priority of economic development has the best chance for success when debated with and against all institutional initiatives at the state board level.

Higher Education Response

The chancellor, working on behalf of the state board, communicates the recommendations to the board members, gets their initial feedback and then sits down with institutional leadership. The first order of business is dealing with the governor's recommendations and getting their input. The legislative concept to eliminate the state board in favor of individual board's demands a separate track for board and institutional discussion. That discussion will begin as soon as the processes are in place responding to the governor's mandates. (Although as suggested in the background, the board is putting out information to dissuade anyone to lobby for the elimination of the board.)

The issues of formula funding, development of outcome measures, increasing resident access and delegation of authority from the board to each institution have major implications for each university and community college. The institutional impacts will vary based on enrollments, budget, missions, location, etc., making the chances of gaining consensus limited. Given that consensus is not likely the next step is to inventory where there are commonalities and where there are differences. The clarification of the differences can provide the board with a means to redesign their own goals and priorities to recognize the similarities and differences.

If, for example, one university can't grow its student population beyond current levels and others can, then should a response based on its institutional mission be made? The growth of student enrollments is even more problematic in that it must be a state resident not nonresidents or international students. The question connected to the governor's 15% growth becomes if one or more institutions can't achieve the desired growth rate must others grow beyond 15% to achieve the overall target? Through the planning process and debate there must first must be realistic enrollment estimates for each institution and if one or more falls short of 15% over the three-year period, then difficult decisions must be made on either inflating measures to 15% overall or justifying a lower number in the final. Neither of the options is good if the 15% rate is hard and fast and allows no leeway for compromise.

Similarly, if not all institutions can assume responsibility of personnel functions currently administered under the board's system office then more than one solution may be justified. In each instance it will be necessary to explain why the governor's original recommendation can't be done and how the higher education's solutions will be best for the citizens of the state. As in the case of enrollment growth rate, if there is no room for allowing some institutions to maintain personnel functions with the system office, then conflict is inevitable.

As in the case of the previous examples the governor's recommendations gives a sense that one size fits all and it is incumbent on higher education to concisely justify solutions that will work for higher education and the state. While it may seem logical for the governor to compromise on the growth rate or decentralizing of functions it may be that the big-P politics is in play. External expectations from the governor with support from the legislature may demand the conditions be met because they don't believe the rationale or simply feel higher educations can and should stretch to limits in growth and oversight. Sometimes the reasons for external decisions can be based on logic and other times simply because powerful legislators are trading one item for another. In those instances where they are targeted as part of a trade, there may be multiple tradeoffs being made between multiple parties.

On the other hand, formula funding can be developed for each type of institution with recognition of differences in mission, enrollments, urban or rural locations, two-year or four-year programs, land grants, doctoral programs, and other specialized academic programming. However, capturing sufficient, high-quality data can be a major stumbling block in truly achieving equitable formulas. Thus, higher education leaders are confronted with finding sufficient data that supports individual institutions but also fits into an overall system strategy. More often than not, state-level formulas are not overly complex in that they are attempting to find some portion of an overall appropriation with the recognition that not all programs can be formula driven. There are land grant programs like agricultural extension, or fringe benefit recommendations, or nonacademic programs that are not subject to a meaningful formula and they are handled separately. In Arizona (Arizona Board of Regents 2012) they had developed a formula that provided increments of funding based on performance for research/service (external research and service funding) and instructional programs (number of degrees awarded and completed student credit hours). There were also base adjustments for cost of living and fringe costs and decision packages that would be considered.

The chancellor develops a timeline for strategic planning efforts with a systemwide committee providing direction and leadership. Each institution has their own committees acting at the direction of the system guidelines but also addressing their own unique expectations. The chancellor directs a president's council comprised of the leaders of each institution as an ongoing resource to share information from the board, the governor's office, the legislature, and the presidents.

The chancellor also builds a lobbying plan including goals and timeline to be coordinated with campus efforts. The intention in this instance is to get as much usable information from the strategic planning process to be shared with the public. Lobbying or the marketing of higher education priorities and outcomes is critical.

The system CFO and a consultant work with institutional financial personnel in creating funding formulas as generated from key indicators or measures of institutional activity. There is a flow of information between the strategic planning committee and the formula development group identifying measures that are important to higher education and can be captured in existing data systems.

As the process evolves, the system strategic planning committee creates strategies formed from board goals, existing strategic directions and plans, outcome measures, and inputs from institutional planning committees. The P and A framework is working through the issues as they arise and as sufficient information is available

The chancellor and institutional presidents, following the initiation of the strategic planning process, begin to lay out the pros and cons for eliminating the board. The chancellor, while conflicted as a leader that will lose a job if the termination occurs, wants to at least pursue some objective assessment of what would be lost and gained if the board was eliminated. The intention is to arm the board with an accurate case for maintaining the system as a viable statewide resource for policy and oversight. As importantly is developing a counterargument of what will happen if the board is disbanded. The process will also enlighten the institutions to the benefits of a state system and ideally get outliers to appreciate their value through specific examples of support. It is anticipated there may be one or two presidents who covertly support board termination.

Applying the Six Components of the SDMM

As outlined in *Planning, Policy, and Politics in Higher Education: Tools to Help Leaders Make Strategic Choices* (Anderes 2016), there are six components to the SDMM. Prior to laying out the scenario the components of strategic thinking, information, and data gathering and analysis, future scans, strategic planning process, transparency, and the P and A framework were defined. The success of the model is built in part on the understanding that components are not completed in successive order but rather are occurring simultaneously and interactively. They will share information with one another throughout a planning process. The component of strategic thinking feeds information into the strategic planning process, supports communications strategies/transparency, and helps refine the planning and assessment framework outputs as it considers how to resolve problems. The strategic planning process shares information with constituencies to ensure transparency, it will use information provided through the P and A framework, it will use strategic thinking in assessment of issues, and it will continuously use information and data driven from institution and system sources.

In advance of developing the alternative, we should summarize the conditions confronted by higher education as posed by the governor and legislature. There are many conditions that must be considered by higher education as they develop responses. The primary basis for higher education's planning will be in response to the multiple demands of the governor. They also must include recent historical losses in funding as a major contributing factor in setting the boundaries of what institutions can do in achieving the mandates of the governor. There are recent changes in the balance of political power in the state that could be influential. The chancellor and board must set their own conditions in how best to plan for and answer the governor's request. They must establish the processes and responses that honor the mission, goals, and strategic directions of higher education as well as the governor's political expectations.

The success of higher education will be in part based on its ability to create a comprehensive strategic planning process that fully utilizes the six components of the SDMM. The outcome of the review will go beyond the single component analysis completed through the P and A framework in prior chapters and offer a more complete assessment using the full SDMM.

Conditions of Scenario

- Public higher education has had state funds cut in the four prior years.
- Recent elections have given the state senate and governor from the same party but different from the four prior years.
- The governor is not recommending increases in the upcoming budget but may do so in the future, depending on the availability of additional revenues.
- The governor seeks higher education support in statewide economic development, increasing resident access (added 15% growth in state residents over three years), developing funding formulae, and creating additional outcome measures.
- The governor would give greater authority to each campus in the areas of personnel and facilities planning (i.e., decentralizing the functions from the system offices to each institution).
- The governor requests that institutions identify administrative functions that could be consolidated.
- The legislature is introducing a bill to eliminate the state board and establish separate boards for the five universities and ten community colleges.
- The chancellor will lead system wide efforts in strategic planning with each institution having its own committee. Lobbying efforts will also be managed through the system chancellor's office.
- The board opposes termination but will consider some delegation of authority and initiatives for increased efficiency. Any lobbying done by internal constituencies supporting the termination of the board will be strongly discouraged.

- Faculty and students are organizing to make sure their thoughts on compensation and tuition respectively are communicated through the internal committees.
- The system chief fiscal officer will work with a consultant and fiscal officers of the campuses in building a funding formula that is reflective of the primary goals of the system and generates funding to accomplish the goals.

SDMM Component Review

Strategic Thinking

There are six elements to strategic thinking and its value to decision makers:

- System and institutional leaders must be committed to strategic thinking and planning.
- Leaders must be enthusiastic in seeking employee thoughts in decision-making processes.
- Leaders must be transparent in all communications with employees on key decisions.
- Employees must accept (ideally embrace) their role in strategic thinking and planning.
- Leadership must be committed to providing employees tools to succeed.
- Leaders must be committed to providing incentives to employees who actively engage in strategic thinking and planning processes.

Employee Support

The scenario offers many points that demand strategic thought. The first point focused on the leader's commitment to strategic thinking and planning actually lays the groundwork for the remaining five points. Employees will know very quickly the degree to which their participation and input is valued. If it is not seen as useful, then points 2 through 6 are irrelevant. In the context of this scenario the chancellor and leaders do seek input from all constituencies in part to get buy-in for the process but also to get ideas that may be incorporated into the development of strategies. The leader's enthusiasm for constituency participation varies across the institutions but is seen as generally positive.

Points 3 through 6 should have occurred prior to the strategic planning process. The concern for employee commitment through the use of incentives and useful tools should have already been in place. If incentives and tools had not been provided, then gaining employee trust and confidence after the fact could be tough to sell. If there was a belief in leadership support for employees, then there would be far greater possibilities for constituent support to the overall process and its outcomes.

Strategic Thinking Throughout the SDMM

Beyond the principles, it should be clear that strategic thought is necessary in every aspect of the model. The first step in the strategic planning process is to develop a "plan to plan." The beginning is characterized as to coming to agreement on what the goals are, who is participating, identifying outcomes and mandates, etc. Strategic thinking in both process and substance is critical.

Leaders and the various planning committees should be thinking strategically in how best to create strategies that respond to the governor's recommendations for downsizing, growing enrollments, supporting state initiatives, and realigning funding approaches. While the leadership makes final decisions on strategies and budgets it relies on the experts within each institution to give their best thoughts on any ramifications or pros and cons, on change.

Strategic thinking should permeate the framing and follow-up for future scans. Perhaps there is no component more reliant on strategic and forward thinking than future scanning. If models attempting to predict the future use only current or historical information and little disruptive or strategic thinking, then the decisions will reflect the past and not address the future.

The P and A framework is a tool that can take existing issues and problems and offer alternatives to leaders based on strategic manipulation of current and future possibilities. The questions are specifically intended to understand what has happened and apply that to the development of strategic directions into the future. Leaders can use information generated from governors and legislative mandates, to strategic plans, future scans, other environmental scans, and the P and A framework to construct strategies and make choices. The success of all the steps relies on strategic thinking.

Information, Data, and Analyses

The lifeblood of any strategic planning process, no matter how limited or expansive, is the information, data, and related analyses identified as necessary for decision makers. The more limited the use of information and analyses, the greater the opportunity for failure in decision-making.

Two questions should be posed in determining the potential success of planning:

- What types and amounts of information are necessary for successful decision-making?
- What is the appropriate infrastructure for collection and analysis of data in a university, community college, and system?

Asking and answering these questions are based on the goals, timing, and desired outcomes of a process. Once it is clear what information is necessary, it is possible to determine the capacity of the infrastructure to collect the data and perform analyses. Policy and financial analyses will flow from the information depending on the sophistication of an information system to collect and compare data.

What types and amounts of information are necessary for successful decision-making?

The maximum amount and quality of information and related an analysis is essential in responding to this scenario. The strategic planning process requires information that allows leaders to take the primary points in the scenario and create analytical resources that respond to each point.

- Clarify institutional goals, priorities, and strategies to ensure compatibility with continued funding inadequacy. (While the governor recommends no funding reduction, mandated costs will be required that dictate funding reductions or reallocations).

Through the knowledge of goals and program priorities decisions can be made on where funding is most and least critical. Decisions can be made on how to shift funds to address a lack of funding. If there are added mandates in utility costs, compensation increases, or other contractual requirements, then leaders can take funds from the least necessary and alter their program outputs.

Growth in enrollments is mandated which requires added funds to support their education. The strategies to reach the 15% increase in resident students has implications for academic program offerings, faculty levels, tuition and fee increases, space availability, and other student support programs.

- Provide financial insights both historically and into the future based on revised goals and program priorities.

The information needed to make the decisions on revising goals and program directions cuts across all programs, academic and administrative. Qualitative analyses of the implications of program reductions due to cutbacks should precede financial modelling. Alternatives should be developed that highlight the budget impacts of how programs may be reduced once program reviews are completed. All of which requires sufficient, accurate, and timely data and related analyses.

- Review existing indicators of performance and develop new outcome measures.

The program information and data required to build a structure of outcome measures is complex. The goal is to develop indicators that measure the quality of faculty, the value of research, the financial viability of an institution, the quantity of enrollments by student type, the quality of students, the quality of an institution based on multiple factors, etc. In this scenario, success will be measured by the capacity to both define and capture information that is critical to enrollment growth, organizational realignments, measures of performance and more.

- Review existing budget methodologies and create a new formula-/ outcome-based alternative.

The type of budget used in higher education may be one or some combination increments of increase or decrease, program based, formula based, and outcome based. In this scenario, the goal is to go fully to a formula-based budget approach. The method requires that there is substantial data that can be defined and captured to measure student access, faculty workload, administrative support costs (public safety, computing, financial functions, library etc.), student support services (counseling, health, etc.), technology programs/costs, etc. Needless to say, ensuring there are common definitions used among all institutions is critical.

- Review student tuition and fee structure and determine if it is an impediment to increasing student access. If it is, what actions are necessary?

The governor seeks to grow student access and as a logical condition the costs can't be so excessive as to deter students from applying. Thus, having a substantial amount of historical data on tuition and fees in conjunction with similar data of peer institutions is one point for review. Also, historical trends in enrollments by student category (resident, nonresident, international student, gender and race, transfers versus freshman, etc.) in combination with demographic data looking into the future are necessary. The comparative use of the data can give indications of how enrollments have varied based on costs over the years relative to peers and can be further refined by looking at population estimates of probable attendees into the future. There are many variables in projecting how students will react to tuition and fees, and they should be included in any information and data analyses.

As suggested the requirement to grow state resident enrollments by 15% over the next three years places an added emphasis on enrollment estimates. However, increasing the number of students requires tuition and state funding. If state funding is not increasing in the first year, then the burden falls on tuition and reallocations from other programs (i.e., reducing other programs in favor of instructing students).

- Identify potential economic development projects that may meet the mutual expectations of the governor and higher education programming.

It is important to seek input from the faculty on the opportunities they may have in building bonds with the state agencies in the arena of economic development. In most instances the ability to create jobs locally and at the state level is a primary indicator of economic development. Faculty have the unique capacity to use research grants from local, state, and federal sources to build programs that will create jobs. They also are experts in many fields and can use that knowledge when working with state officials on projects or initiatives that benefit the state.

What is the appropriate structure for collecting and analyzing information at the system, university, and community college?

The second primary element of successfully supporting a strategic planning process is defining information and data needs and having certainty in identifying accurate and timely data. It is also necessary to collect sufficient amounts of information to draw conclusions and have the tools to manipulate, aggregate, and estimate to the expectations of higher education decision makers.

It is important to have the most current tools for assessing data and building reports. The need for an information system that can maintain large amounts of data and other forms of information that can be easily compared over years of activity in very finite detail is essential. The technical capacity to construct a data system is one part of the equation in having a successful information and data system. The second is the analytical capacity through a central institutional research and analysis office to define what is needed and to assess its meaning (with experts in the field) for discussion in strategic planning processes. The data, analyses, and reports then become part of the SDMM and interactively addressed through strategic thinking, strategic planning process, future scans, and the P and A framework.

Future Scans—Nationally and Globally

Scanning the future is intended to give leaders an ability to match their current goals, actions, and perspectives, with events that may occur in the future. The future will always be speculative, but all planning is speculative even if it attempts to divine actions only one or two years into the future. If decisions are made based on the past or the current conditions, then much will be missed.

Not long ago there was only minor interest in following what happened throughout the world in higher education beyond the common research projects of faculty or academic relationships in like disciplines. The rapid transfer of information through technological advances has created opportunities for all sectors of our country in learning from their counterparts throughout the world. At the same time the changes in economic, social, educational, and governmental structures and political alignments across the world have influenced leaders in all sectors to look beyond their geographical and historical boundaries. They are now looking to see if there are innovations or disruptions that they should consider to the advantage of their constituencies.

Future scanning is important in a number of the SDMM components. Strategic thinking must have some capacity to look into the future and make judgments about strategies that may or may not be viable. The strategic planning process can only be effective in offering final strategies and plans when it has inputs that assume events and conditions in the future. What can be expected for growth of students, academic program enhancements, creative funding options, changes on the international stage that impact higher education, translations of disruptions in social, medical and technology affecting higher education, and on and on. The P and A framework can use the scanned information and bridge from the problems occurring currently with visions of the future.

In this scenario, all the conditions require a connection between what is occurring now with students (focus on growth), funding (formula development), economic development (support state initiatives), politics (governor and legislature), and organizational change (decentralizing administrative functions) and what may occur in the future. Each of the governor's recommendations demand an assessment of how successful decisions will be in the future if they are or are not enacted as requested. Without a focus on the future, any solutions will be subject to criticism and eventually be seen as short-sighted and rooted in the past.

Strategic Planning

A comprehensive strategic planning process is indispensable in making well informed strategic choices. The more robust the planning process the greater the opportunity for addressing constituent concerns. One excellent framework can be found in the book *Strategic Planning for the Public and Non-Profit Organization* by John Bryson in 2011. It is a ten-step process that if followed is a clear path to making thoughtful decisions. The ten steps are as follows:

- Develop an initial agreement on the strategic planning process—plan for planning.

- Clarify the mandates—what are the expectations that should be addressed?
- Review and clarify the missions of the organization.
- Complete a comprehensive assessment of internal and external environments.
- Identify strategic issues through multiple sources.
- Formulate strategies.
- Finalize strategies, review overall plan, and adopt.
- Describe the new organization of the future.
- Implement the plan.
- Reassess the strategic plan and planning process.

Needless to say, a strategic planning process that follows the steps outlined above will be demanding yet very productive.

It goes without saying that the first step of planning to plan is extremely important. If the plan does not include one or more of the governor's requested items, it immediately loses its value internally and externally. As an example, if strategic planning does not incorporate a thorough review of formula budget development or development of outcome measures it will be seen externally as intentionally avoiding an expectation of the governor. The only outcome of avoiding one of the requests is to accentuate its absence and place an even higher value on its completion in the future. It may even be a catalyst for the governor and legislature to mandate budget formulas without input from higher education or simply to reduce funding as a punishment. It is incumbent on higher education to complete all items requested or suffer the consequences in even harsher ways.

It may be that there is disagreement on how, when, and what level higher education is going to comply with the requests, but that should be acknowledged along with the rationale as to why they are not being pursued as suggested by the governor.

Bryson's second step of clarifying mandates would include those items identified by the governor and internal expectations to meet commitments already in place. Commitments such as support for higher utility costs or contractual expenditures for compensation, additional financial aid fund, or other binding agreements. Other legislative mandates might be to provide required reports on personnel information, organizational policies, financial information and other periodic and one-time analyses of requested information.

In this scenario, the legislative bill to eliminate the statewide board would gain immediate action within the full strategic planning process although separate from the governor's request.

The review of mission and clarifying organizational value of the system and institutions sets the foundation for all the remaining planning. There must be an in-depth understanding and system agreement on the vision, strategic directions, and values before any of the questions raised by the governors can be answered.

The legislative bill eliminating the board offices is particularly significant in first assessing the value of the board and its statewide policy role. What is the perceived value if eliminated and what new functions and activities would each institution have to assume (i.e., what added programs and costs would they have to support)? In times of declining resources and external requirements driving more scrutiny and higher expectations, there must be absolute clarity in vision, mission, and value of each institution.

Higher education leaders may view the requests of the governor and legislature to be of such significance that they have to rethink system and institutional missions. The additional external mandates, with no accompanying funds and on the heels of four years of reductions, establish a red line for institutions and the system. A redesign of the system to redistribute functions even in a minor way would require that the implications for the funding and programs of the institutions receive the full attention and input of all leaders from the system and institutions.

Step 3 becomes perhaps the most critical step in that it recasts a new foundation for each institution that permanently alters the programs and services it offers to students. How many students will be served at what locations under what revised missions and recalibrated funding levels. If the system and institutions went in the direction of redesign, the use of the full SDMM becomes even more critical.

The fourth step is the most intense of the ten steps. It demands a deep dive into all environmental conditions that can affect public higher education. The third step gives certainty to the directions of higher education, while the fourth step leaves no stone unturned in assessing how internal and external environments act and interact to all conditions they do or may confront. The component of information and data analysis is essential in giving leaders the reports, assessment and analyses they need to make decisions. Also, the information provided through future scans creates awareness beyond current boundaries of thought and action.

It is in this step that connection of the process with the P and A framework is in full force. The leaders and their staffs should be filtering all the major issues through the questions raised in the P and A framework for as much clarity as possible.

The specific issues and findings and recommendations on formula development will be generated by a separate committee, which in turn will feed the findings into the overall planning process. The planning process will subject the formula findings to the full analysis through the P and A framework to provide cross-verification of information used in the full process and validity of the recommendations. It will run funding models to determine the implications of the differing variables on the amount of funds needed to fully fund the formula (this analysis of the formula would be done in conjunction with the system-level committee developing the formula).

The other requests will follow the same pattern of review and assessment to determine how they fit into the bigger strategic directions of each institution and system. The demand for student growth to reach an additional 15% resident students (students from the state) in the next three years affects the existing goals and outcomes. Is that target possible and if it is what will it cost to reach that level of students in terms of added faculty and support staff?

The development of outcome measures will require an in-depth review of what the driving forces are in the major programs and subprograms. How do we measure student support services, research programs, health and safety programs, instructional course work, faculty productivity, quality of services, etc.? Each area that will have outcomes will have multiple variables that will have to be assessed within the system wide environment and within each institutional environment to determine what works best in representing the programs workload.

The shifting of organizational responsibilities from the system to institutions is another request which demands close attention by the system and each institution. The environmental analyses that characterize this step should include a review of the responsibilities of the personnel functions and facilities planning to determine the implications of transferring from the system to each institution. What are the personnel and facilities planning functions or responsibilities currently done at the system? What are the system resources used to support the functions currently? Does each institution have parallel personnel and facilities functions on campus that can absorb the tasks? If not would staffing and other resources be necessary to startup the functions? If an institution does not have the resources to accept the functions should consideration be given to continue the services at the system?

The internal and external environmental analyses should be able to ask and answer the questions as one set of information for the strategic planning committees to consider when responding to the governor's recommendations.

The termination of the system also requires an intense review of the issues surrounding the role and responsibilities of the system and board. The board and system offer a statewide perspective on higher education and as such can provide solutions to the issues the state confronts with a certainty in support from all universities and community colleges. The statewide perspective and support go away when there are fifteen separate boards offering their individual responses to policy issues. Issues of significance including student access, cost of education, and tuition and fee costs will be now derived from individual campuses. Legal issues such as gun control and rape on campus won't benefit from a single statewide perspective. Funding equity among state supported institutions will be far more difficult to define when a state board no longer exists.

The environmental analysis would have to clarify how each institution would have to assume the reporting and interface requirements of their campus for budget, planning, legal issues, capital planning, financial oversight, etc., with all the various state agencies. From the state perspective it would now get fifteen different responses for everything that they would have to pay equal attention to as opposed to the overall summary efforts of the system.

(It is assumed that state-level offices will not identify new resources necessary to provide the quality control currently offered by a system. The typical mantra of doing more with less would be the state-level commitment)

The fifth step involves the identification of strategic issues flowing from the environmental assessments. The issues become a focus for leaders as they consider the implications of the governor's request and the legislative bill. However, there are countless other issues that may or may not be connected to the executive and legislative concerns.

The strategic issues of enrollment growth, organizational realignments, economic development projects, formula funding, and creating new outcome measures are significant by themselves. However, as the system and each institution attempt to respond to those requests they will also be looking at, in some depth, at tuition and fee structures, faculty compensation, and faculty availability for new/expanded programs. Also, they will have to assess facilities planning for current and future demands, support for student technology, counseling, improvement of student health services, etc.

No less attention can be paid to the elimination of unspecified programs due to no increase in funding. The strategic issues must be considered in processes that will assess their value relative to other policies and priorities. Thus, while it is important to address the governor's request to increase student enrollments by 15% over the next three years, it must be done in the context of institutional goals and priorities.

If increasing student enrollment requires new faculty and support services and the governor is not recommending any new funding, should not higher education clarify how that will negatively affect other programs? It may be necessary to eliminate various courses or administrative programs to shift funding to teaching and raise tuition and fees. The net effect of increasing the students cost of education could be to place even greater pressure on students in being able to graduate on time.

Generally speaking, in many instances, higher education leaders will try to acknowledge the expectations of the governor and implement programs to increase enrollments by 15%. In the long run, it is the best policy for leaders to be on the right side of the governor. However, it is incumbent to be absolutely clear in how leaders are making decisions to the benefit of the governor's agenda but not necessarily that of higher education. There should be an understanding of what may be lost when submitting to the expectations of external authorities, in this case the governor.

As might expected, strategic issues are created through multiple layers of strategic thinking. Even if issues are generated by an external authority, higher education leaders must take those ideas and filter them through the missions, goals, and priorities of higher education. The governor's concept of outcome measures may be very different as interpreted and developed by higher education. The strategic issues would be run through the P and A framework with outputs shared with the strategic planning committees. It is the whole of the SDMM that must be utilized in the process and substance of the issues raised by the governor and legislature.

Step 6 is the point at which strategies can be formulated. The intense assessment of the environments along with the identification of strategic issues offers sufficient background to build preliminary directions. The strategic issues and potential directions can be debated by all constituencies to give leaders the full scope of the strengths and weakness of each strategy.

In this scenario, as mentioned in step 5, the strategic issues are driven from an external agenda and from internal expectations of internal constituencies. One external requirement by the governor seeks higher education to develop more outcome measures as a means to determine if various objectives are being achieved. The guiding strategic issue would be measuring performance to determine success or failure.

Formulation of a strategy would include identifying measures that could determine success in what leadership feels is most important including enrollment growth by type of student by program and research growth in specific areas of emphasis. Also, the number of students graduating in four years, faculty student ratios by level of instruction, budget expenditures per FTE student or faculty member, and number of students per academic counselor a few other areas for measurement.

As the outcome measures are more narrowly defined in addressing the governor's requirement to increase student enrollments, the capacity to capture historical and current data is critical.

Students may be a combination of full-time, on scholarship, part-time, male/female/trans, Hispanic, African American, Asian, Caucasian, native, international, state resident, nonresident, and so forth. The numbers by types of student becomes important as leaders look at their institutional profile and how that relates to the overall environmental mix they are serving. In the case of the governor's mandate, the total state resident population is to increase by 15% over three years, which for the sake of more background, represents 75% of the total student body. Three quarters of the population comes from the state suggesting that the new or revised enrollment growth strategy must focus on what most important to state residents.

As can be seen, the formulation of a strategy demands a deep understanding of student attendance patterns, demographic projections, tuition and fee barriers, creative marketing based on current student expectations (i.e., enhanced technology resources, graduate in four years, available student counseling, etc.), and much more.

Thus, taking the governor's basic request to increase student resident enrollment by 15% requires much more analysis of multiple factors or variables. All committees must examine the same resources and reports as they seek to formulate a clear strategy in addressing the governor's growth requirement. The strategy must encompass the full range of decisions that need to be made on enrollments with the governor's recommendation as one of the primary outcomes.

The SDMM suggest that as strategies are formulated they be assessed through the P and A framework. That is, the range of questions embedded in the framework is used to identify if there are any hidden concerns that should be raised for deeper inquiry. If by applying the P and A framework there are alternatives that run counter to current thinking, then there should be an examination of the pros and cons of competing issues. That analysis should be filtered through the full resources of the strategic planning process to gain some clarity and consensus or further division on the related strategic issues.

Again, the strategic planning processes, continuous strategic thinking, the P and A framework, availability of useful data and analyses including future scans all combine in the SDMM to give leaders the best opportunity to formulate useful and timely strategies.

Step 7 is finalizing all strategies, review the overall plan and adopt a final plan. It is at this point that all constituencies would have given their input and had a chance to react to the strategies formulated in step 6. If there were concerns by the students that tuition and fees remained vulnerable to increases as addressed in steps 4-6, there would be an opportunity to offer final thoughts. Typically, no changes would be made at this point unless there had been some major over sight in the logic of the strategic position. If the final plan raised concerns about the capacity to grow student access into the future (the governor-mandated growth), then strategies outlining what growth was possible and why it would make sense would be the basis for responding to the governor.

The strategies laid out in the plan would reflect a full awareness of constituent internal and external expectations but not necessarily support all aspirations. It is extremely important that any public plan expresses not only what is supported but is also thoughtful in clarifying what is not a priority. It is useful for constituencies that have priorities that were not supported be aware of why they were not included and if there are possibilities for future consideration.

In this step, it is essential for leaders to fully outline the system and institutional recommendations. Each institutional leader should be able to identify specific points where there will be changes in how programs and services are delivered. Those changes that may require staffing or faculty reductions, elimination of programs or additions of new tasks will be of greatest interest to all constituencies. They will need to know how they are affected and the processes and timing of how change will be implemented.

The transparency of laying out final decisions and offering opportunities for questions is important for constituencies. There may not be agreement with the decisions, but the process will have allowed for input and debate. Similarly, the board should be providing feedback to the public on the findings and recommendations with attention to addressing the governors and legislative requests/demands. The governor's office should have been in the communications loop as the strategic planning process was moving through stages of development and given opportunities for input. The final product should not be a surprise to any constituencies.

As the plan is laid out for public review it will be subject to analyses by external leaders that have an interest in supporting or opposing the final plan. If from the perspective of some legislative leaders that the plan and strategies did not adequately commit to organizational changes, or a robust number of outcome measures, or requested student growth, then the opposition will begin efforts to discredit the recommendations. It will be a long session for higher education leaders.

Step 8 offers the opportunity for leaders to discuss how the system and institutions may have changed strategically and functionally in the new strategic plan. It is separated from step 7 because the focus is on the specifics of change and how the adopted plan has different meanings for implementation for each institution.

As the plan is taken to internal and external constituencies, the discussion of how the system and institutions may have changed is critical. The requirements for institutions to assume more responsibilities from the system means changes in what services are now carried out by the institution and system. More responsibilities will often require more funding, staffing, training, space, etc., thus having an impact on local planning and budgets.

If the system is terminated, then the magnitude of change is substantially greater. Each institution must identify and redefine the current policies, academic programs, administrative and legal aspects, and activities overseen by a system for their own university or community college. They will have their own boards and must be responsive to the expectations of a new governing body while building a much closer relationship with the governor's office, the legislature, and other state agencies.

The implementation of the plan offers more of a challenge than many might think. The system and institutions must coordinate their efforts on the timing and explanations of the implications of each recommended change. It is particularly important for each institution to lay out the changes in a public forum for all constituencies to participate.

The system must provide institutions with a plan that identifies a timeline and process for implementing specific initiatives. The timeline will reflect a range of dates based on the capacity for each institution to implement change. If it takes a community college longer than a university to assume the centralized functions, then it will be acknowledged by the system schedule. There will be a final date for all institutions to reach when all implementation should be complete, but flexibility will be provided within the boundaries of the beginning and closing dates. The system will also lay out the major program and organizational changes affecting each institution and get feedback on how they will be accomplished by each campus. If one institution is going to require added staff to handle the expanded responsibilities and others can absorb them into existing functions, then the one institution will have to offer a plan on timing and resource needs to accomplish the change. Each university and community college will have to translate the realignments into a work plan that draws in the appropriate internal constituencies who will be responsible for the implementation.

The final step is to reassess the strategic plan and planning process. It is necessary to establish mechanisms that evaluate the progress made in achieving the goals and measures identified in the strategic plan. The degree to which systems, institutions, or programs meet their goals is a statement on the validity of their plans as presented to internal and external constituencies. The greater the accuracy of the planning strategies and outcomes that greater their opportunity for acceptance in the future.

The process of planning requires follow-up as well. The questions that should be asked include the following:

- Were all constituencies pleased with their level of participation in various planning phases?
- Did each step in the process allow for maximum amount of input?
- Were there any complaints from members of the committees that should be considered in the future (e.g., timing, constituent participation, availability of requested information, leadership feedback)?
- Could the environmental assessments be improved—i.e., were there other sources of information that should be considered in the future?
- Were the communications strategies effectively managed between all constituencies?
- Were the processes considered transparent to internal and external constituencies?
- Did leadership fully utilize the P and A framework in their analyses? Was it considered useful?

Transparency

If constituencies are aware of forums for debate on key issues, can offer input prior to decisions being made, and can offer reactions after decisions are made, then the process was transparent. If it is any less than that then constituencies will have a basis from which they can protest and work against leadership decisions.

It is important for leaders to follow four principles for success.

- **Process:** All constituencies should be aware of the goals of any strategic planning process and how they participate in the process.
- **Participation:** All constituencies should be aware of how they can individually and collectively participate in a process. Will there be forums for discussion and debate? Will there be opportunities to discuss and react to preliminary findings? Will there be opportunities to participate on select committees that are established to deal with given aspects of the issues under consideration? Will there be mechanisms to react to and influence decisions in their final stages?
- **Timing:** The transparency of timing can be as important as the actual substance under discussion. If participation is limited based on timing, then the process may be viewed as weighted toward one outcome. What is an overall time-line for a process? What are the key intermediate dates for decision-making? When is participation allowed within the process and on what topics? Can additional forums or committee meetings be considered if the current schedule is difficult for constituents to attend?
- **Actions:** There are multiple points for action in a strategic planning process. As in Bryson's ten-step planning process, there are numerous points at which actions are taken to accept or deny various findings and recommendations. Is there an agreement on the plan to plan? Is there an agreement on the implications of the environmental scans—i.e., do institutions support the assessments? Are the mandates understood by all constituencies? Have the key strategic issues been identified? What strategies must move forward for leadership consideration? Is the plan for implemen-

tation clear and understood by all leaders—i.e., are they committed to make it successful?

Transparency is often viewed as a secondary or less important step in many strategic planning processes. If it is not given the attention it deserves, then all the planning done in more closed settings will be disputed by those who were not allowed to participate and certainly by those who don't benefit from the outcomes of the process.

Planning and Assessment Framework

A key and unique component of the SDMM, the P and A framework acts as a vehicle to raise questions about the issues in a consistent format. The intent is to force leaders and their staffs to pursue issues in-depth and in a consistent manner. As we have seen in prior chapters, the use of the P and A framework was instructive in understanding the implications of each of the scenarios. Its value to the SDMM is not as a final point for making a decision but rather as a resource to be used in the overall strategic planning process. It supplied analyses including alternatives that could be used in conjunction with other sources such as financial reports, committee feedback, constituent submissions, external views, etc., from which leaders could construct final positions. Also, the P and A framework could offer an analysis on a given topic or issue and revise the analysis as the strategic planning committee had more information.

The P and A framework would be particularly useful in a number of areas of this scenario including an assessment of any changes in mission or values of institutions, the termination of the board, the implications of a new funding formula, the shifting of functions from the system to each institution, the implications of no enrollment growth, etc.

Applying the Planning and Assessment Framework

1. What is the problem? What creates instability? Is there
   agreement on the problem?

The governor is requiring higher education to grow its enrollments, use a different method of funding, use a different method of accountability (outcome measures), and support the state's economic development efforts, all within the context of no additional funding. The legislature is recommending that the statewide governing board be eliminated in favor of individual boards.

The response to the problems is to create strategic planning processes that go beyond just the requirements of the governor and to build a more holistic approach to the expectations. That is, if enrollment growth is required, what does that mean for enrollments, faculty staffing levels, funding estimates, classroom space, and support programs for students, etc., by institution? In other words, enrollment growth isn't simply a unidimensional initiative but rather an action with multiple dimensions and impacts that will vary by institutional mission.

Does this create instability? It may create instability depending on how the governor delivers the message to the public. If it is suggested that higher education is not meeting its commitments to statewide goals, then it is threatening. If public statements are given in a positive manner highlighting the supportive efforts of higher education, then it will appear less threatening. If the planning processes look closely at how they will fund new services related to student growth, then any discussions of reallocating existing resources will raise concerns.

2. What examples contribute to the problem? What is the
   magnitude of the problem?

The examples include those items requested by the governor as mentioned in question 1. The development of the funding formula, economic development initiatives, development of outcome measures, and growing enrollments are the most-obvious examples. Secondary examples include the necessity to raise tuition and fees to partially fund student growth and the availability of monies for additional faculty and any compensation increases.

The political fallout of the legislative bill to eliminate the board and create new institutional boards would be at minimum unsettling and at its worst highly divisive. It would be divisive throughout the state in that many would not want to lose a statewide perspective on public higher education, while others would be more sympathetic to locating boards locally and reducing centralized costs. On an internal level many institutions would be happy to shed an outside bureaucratic authority like the state board but then would be faced with creating many of the same policies and regulatory oversight through their local board. It is likely that the governor and legislature will require the same types of accountability on access, quality, funding, support for statewide issues such as economic development, and more as institutions gain independence. However, the independence will be limited.

The severity of problem and its many connecting factors is quite significant. Anytime you are looking at financial stress, organizational restructuring, student growth, and demands for a new way of funding the pressures are extreme.

3. What is the origin of the current examples? What caused the problem?

The state had been reducing the higher education funding for a number of years thus compounding the difficulties in addressing the governor's mandates. The fact that there was no funding reduction seemed like a positive given the recent history, but it still meant that tuition or reallocations were needed to move forward.

The requirement for a new funding model originated out of the sense that current methodologies did not accurately reflect needs. The outcome measures came about because the existing measures of success were insufficient. The expectation of growing enrollments originated from the governor's desire to maximize access for state residents which could have been based on demographics and politics.

All constituencies agreed that the continuing reductions have spawned more and more finite requirements meant to justify the use of existing funds and where possible give rationale for reducing funds.

4. Is there a historical precedent or relevance? Does the precedent connect with current issues?

The state had been reducing state taxes and related revenues for years thus the continuing cuts to higher education. It is doubtful that there are any occurrences in history of the magnitude of continuing funding losses that could make a useful comparison. The crush of cuts stemming from the great recession beginning in 2008 and policies of limiting taxation have no meaningful historical parallel.

While they can learn from the past the magnitude of loss demands solutions that are more severe and damaging than ever before. A redefinition of mission, goals, programs, services, and the basic value of higher education are required.

5. Which constituencies are most affected? Do all feel there is a problem? What is the relative state of each?

All constituencies are affected. All should be actively engaged in the strategic planning forums, committees, and processes to listen closely to each other while fully detailing their own positions and priorities.

Students will pay more and not see any benefit. Faculty will have a greater workload and may not receive any new compensation. Leaders at the system level will be fighting for each institution but also their own existence. Institutional leaders will be debating about their programs and budget within their own university or community college but will also have to compete with their colleagues for recognition at the system level.

As leaders discuss the key aspects of the planning process, it should be apparent that all constituencies will benefit from working with one another. As seen in experiences in earlier chapters, when students and faculty work with one another in concert with the institutional leaders on the primary priorities, all have a greater opportunity to benefit. The united front of system and institutional leaders goes much farther in convincing the governor and legislature that higher education is resolute on its positions and willing to fight for those positions.

6. Provide alternatives or actions on how to strategically prepare for and address problems in the future.

One alternative will be structured to maximize the capacity of leaders to respond to the governor and legislature, but within a comprehensive plan that clarifies the major goals, strategies, and priorities of higher education. The achievement of the governor's mandates will come at a cost. The implications of those costs on current and future funding requests, student enrollments, public expectations, qualitative concerns, and student tuition and fees will be provided in graphic detail. There will be no doubt that as efforts are made to address the governor's mandates higher education leadership will have expectations of the governor in supporting the full higher education agenda. It can be said that both sides will have measures of accountability that can be shared with the public.

Alternative—Background

In an earlier section of this chapter, higher education laid out a response to the governor's recommendations. The response provides background for the development of an alternative focused on process; mission, goals, and outcomes; organizational change; and budget realignments. It also must consider new marketing strategies, more detailed accountability expectations within and outside of higher education, and a general willingness to readapt to external demands but with conditions.

The alternative should be responsive to the external parties of the governor, the legislature, and the public while also being true to the goals of public higher education. The first step is to understand the big picture as it relates to internal and external constituencies. The macro level problem, per the P and A framework, is that external authorities mandate change without an awareness of the implications of impacting the mission, goals and plans of higher education. They demand more from faculty, students, and leaders but give nothing of value in return (unless not reducing funding is now a positive value). The demands superficially speak to efficiency in the delivery of services and serving more students. Unfortunately, the net effect is providing the public with programs and service that have and will continue to diminish significantly or simply go the way of the horse and buggy, thus cheating the citizens of the best education possible.

The bottom line for higher education then is to offer solutions that put an emphasis on providing the best programs and services to the public but with a warning that the product they are offering while accredited is devalued by the continuing neglect of the state. The question then becomes do the citizens want an average education that offers the basics but may not challenge students in a way that they can maximize their learning opportunities. It is very difficult for higher education leaders to say they are offering a product that isn't of the highest excellence. However, unless there is an annual redesign of academic and administrative service and reallocated funding, it is inevitable that some programs no longer have the quality of faculty or support services they might have had years earlier. They continue to be sufficient but not excellent.

Alternative

Only one alternative is offered given the extreme nature of the governor's request. It is seen as the only viable option under the past, present, and future diminishment of public higher education. It pushes back on the governor's expectations to the extent that there is no state-funding commitment, yet high demands for growth that will cost money. The ideas of student growth, developing outcome measures, and creating a new funding methodology can be supported but with conditions.

The alternative must begin with the condition that public higher education has regularly readapted to continuing funding shortfalls but not without some loss of capacity to develop new strategies and programs better suited for the future. It isn't an admission that programs are not of value but rather an honest statement borne out by years of underfunding. How long can programs be cut or lost without some impact on what is available to students? If the students are the primary "customers," then what programs and services are offered, how often they are offered, and at what cost are important factors when they are deciding where to attend and if they can attend based on those factors.

The idea of pushing back on the governor's request, at least to the extent that higher education must express its frustration with diminished support, has become more acceptable even necessary within the history and context of this scenario.

The chancellor and board have agreed that they need to offer solutions for the governor's request but use it as an opportunity to tell more of the higher education story. The story will consist of the damage to higher education in recent years coming from lost state funding. It will also tell the plight of student, who has been forced to assume a greater share of the cost of a public higher education. Questions of access based on cost, limited course availability, extended time to graduate, technology limitations, and student health offerings will be raised on the diminished quality of student programming.

Governor's Expectations / Higher Education's Strategic Responses

The request to grow **resident student enrollments** by 15% will be conditioned on the limitations of student cost. Without any new state funds, tuition will have to increase simply to maintain existing services. The increase may be further discouragement to continuing students and force prospective students to seek other options.

The need to develop a **new funding model** will be positioned as a means to offer a formula that, if fully funded, will improve higher education. The improvement will be based on attracting additional state dollars that can limit tuition increases while offering students more options. The need to reflect a formula that provides more than current funding will be a point for dispute with external authorities. If the formula eventually approved by the legislature is tied to actual expenditures, which are only a reflection of the past, then higher education's capacity to grow through state funds is nonexistent.

The development of **outcome measures** will be seen as an opportunity to highlight key indicators of not only successful programs but also as variables of a funding formula. The connection of performance and funding is a logical relationship for higher education leaders and external authorities.

Economic development initiatives should be the easiest of all the governor's requests assuming universities and community colleges don't have to reallocate their resources to state needs without something of value in return. It may be an opportunity to get a concession as part of the overall agreement.

The shifting of two functions of **personnel and facilities planning** from the system to each institution should be supported to the extent that there are no added costs to each institution. It would be one of the items that if an agreement could be reached with external authorities, it might be stopgap to the full termination of the board (or at least a deferral until some later time).

The **continuation of the board** should be actively defended with a lobbying effort to highlight what will be lost in oversight including statewide priority setting, access/enrollment planning statewide, funding equity, quality review of programs and services, and a forum for the public to discuss and debate the key higher education issues of the time.

There is a significant amount of work that must take place at the system and its institutions to build the story of how relative decline in recent years can be turned into accessible and high-quality education for state residents and others. While many governors and legislators do not like to look beyond their state boundaries, there is a large amount of data that leaders can use to prove their case using peer institutional data. The combination of historical information on funding decline, tuition increases, faculty compensation, enrollment limitations, etc., with what is happening with comparable peers can provide a picture that is hard to dispute.

As stated earlier, there will be significant big-P politics involved in any new major directions mandated for higher education. It is particularly true that the public may get concerned when a formula or other initiatives require more state support and highlight the damage done to the state higher education programs if not funded. There are very little legislators like less than appearing to be overtly against students and higher education.

The institutions should have dealt with the internal politics through the planning processes. However, there will be constituencies that may feel they didn't get the visibility they deserve and will continue to agitate for more funding or recognition. It is a normal reaction to any planning processes that there are those that see themselves as having "lost" and will want to make sure leaders are aware of their feelings and continuing expectations.

The planning outlined in the scenario, with the limitations of avoiding too much detail suggest that the strategic planning processes were thorough. The strategies developed were an outcome of strategic thinking, planning, ongoing assessment, and coordination between and among the system and institutions. The use of the SDMM offered an in-depth and consistent approach to identification of key issues/problems and addressing them in a comprehensive and transparent way.

Politics and Constituencies: Making Strategic Choices

One of the primary intentions of the book has been to raise the idea of politics as a major factor in decision-making. The political influences were seen as external to higher education on the public scale of political parties. The party politics was represented by elected legislative representatives making decisions based on a calculus of their ideology and the perception of the electorates support for positions or votes on important topics. While the term *political* can be seen at times as a negative, particularly if a decision goes against a constituency position, it generally can be characterized as the will of a big-P party or subset with the enough votes to be successful. Thus, the balance of power that shifts over time among big-P political actors is a known and should be included in any decision-making calculations made by higher education leaders.

Similarly, internal politics among numerous constituencies in higher education, all competing for a priority position in decision-making, is common. It was and is the politics of competing groups and individuals seeking to emphasize their values and goals as paramount in their institution. The faculty, staff, students, and institutional leaders representing a wide array of programs and priorities argued for their share of visibility and resources. As argued at the beginning of the book, the ability to successfully achieve some of the objectives while moving forward should have been a priority of every constituency. The acceptance of even a few positive outcomes with a sense of defeat would avoid the reality of many constituencies competing intensely for few resources.

In both the internal and external environments, there was much debate, dissent, cooperation, conflict, and compromise over issues of great importance and issues of little importance. The degree to which any single constituency had its goals supported was dependent on timing; leadership from the constituency, institution, and system, and funding availability. Also important were goals coinciding with the issues of the day, luck, thoughtful justification, external support or simply avoidance of external opposition, and other factors that would vary year to year.

While an understanding the politics of internal and external constituency interaction was a primary goal so was the application of a tool that provided a capacity to make more strategic choices. The SDMM is a tool that if used correctly can organize leaders and their institutions in a way that maximizes the ability of constituencies to work cooperatively on the most difficult problems. It recognizes the expectations of all constituencies, ensures input, emphasizes as much transparency as possible, and develops solutions that will address the most demanding requirements of both internal and external parties.

The SDMM is relatively simple in concept. Certainly, everyone thinks strategically. Of course, information and reports are necessary. Undoubtedly a strategic planning process makes imminent sense. The questions raised in the P and A framework are basic and well defined. Who would argue that we must look into the future? And transparency should always be a goal. Again, the model is simple in concept.

The complexity of the model comes into play when planners and leaders don't take each of the components seriously. They want to find short cuts to avoid either time or resource constraints. The question becomes which component do you eliminate or limit? If you move through the initial steps of creative thinking about the problems and defining outcomes quickly and avoid some of the early steps of the strategic planning process, you are doomed to failure. Failure would be characterized by not knowing or considering mandates, not thinking in-depth about vision, goals, and strategic directions of each institution, and not maximizing the amount and quality of analyses informing leaders.

Ultimately, the strategies that would be under consideration would be limited by the amount and quality of meaningful strategic thought and related information resources informing the decisions. That is, while decisions can be made, they will be shallow in their content and subject to criticism by many.

One could find countless examples of how, if any, one of the components is not fully integrated into a planning process, then one or more constituencies will be justified in questioning the entire process. A lack of transparency will negate much good work if there isn't sufficient communication and input. Limited data will mean a limited basis for findings, recommendations, and solutions. Misuse of the P and A framework will render possible alternatives as suspect and open to criticism. A lack of thoughtful exchanges on the key goals and strategic directions among institutional leaders and system leaders will cause confusion and distrust on what is to be accomplished and when accomplishments are expected.

The SDMM is not a tool that makes decisions for leaders. It is a vehicle to fully organize and inform all constituencies of how to address and respond to current problems. It takes the data, inputs, reports, constituency expectations, external requirements, leadership directives, board goals, and more to shape potential strategies for leadership consideration and action.

As a tool, the SDMM will be best used in the following situations:

- Strategic thought is actively pursued throughout the institution with an awareness of what is happening in the institution and in the external environment.
- Data, information, and analytical reporting are fully developed and integrated into an institution's ongoing decision-making processes.
- Future scanning fully defined and operationalized in institutions to ensure that all decisions have context of the past, present, and future.
- Transparency eliminates any opportunities for constituencies to say they were not allowed to participate in the process.
- Strategic planning, as the core of the SDMM, is the means of pulling together the thought, organization, and implementation of all the SDMM components.
- The planning and assessment framework is the qualitative control of the SDMM in that it demands answers to all difficult questions before any alternatives are made.

Institutions and systems must fully commit to the principles of the model to get the greatest value. The greater the commitment, the less simple it seems and yet the greater the benefit to leaders and their institutions.

In *Planning, Policy and Politics in Higher Education: Tools to Help Leaders Make Strategic Choices* (Anderes 2016), I evaluated the use of the model in assessing an issue/scenario on governance. The point of the evaluation exercise was to generally assess the value of the SDMM in decision-making but also highlight the necessity of all six components working in conjunction with one another. The evaluation reflected that decision-making was greatly enhanced and its success was and is based on how much effort and resources leaders are willing to commit in developing and implementing a comprehensive planning approach.

REFERENCES

Anderes, Tom. *Planning, Policy, and Politics in Higher Education: Tools to Help Leaders Make Strategic Choices*. New York: Page Publishing, 2016.

Arizona Board of Regents. "Arizona university system performance-based funding model." 2012.

———. "Budget summary request." AZRegents.edu. 2015.

Brewer, Jan (Arizona governor). "The four cornerstones of reform: Building a framework of effective and responsible governance" (2013 policy agenda). 2013.

———. "The four cornerstones of reform: guiding Arizona to a more prosperous future" (2014 policy agenda). 2014.

Bryson, John M. *Strategic Planning for Public and Nonprofit Organizations*, Fourth Edition. San Francisco, CA: Jossey-Bass, 2011.

"Constituency." The Free Dictionary, http://www.thefreedictionary.com/constituency. Accessed November 21, 2016.

"Constituency." *Merriam-Webster*, http://www.merriam-webster.com/dictionary/constituency. Accessed (November 21, 2016.

Cowan, Kristina. "Higher education's higher accountability." American Council on Education, Winter Student Issues, 2013.

Hearn, James C. "Outcome-based funding in historical and comparative context." Lumina Foundation Issue Papers, 2015.

Miller, James L. "State budgeting for higher education: the use of formula and cost analysis." Ann Arbor: Institute of Public Administration, the University of Michigan, 1964.

REFERENCES

"Politics." *Merriam-Webster*, http://www.merriam-webster.com/dictionary/politics. Accessed November 10, 2016.

"Politics." The Free Dictionary, http://www.thefreedictionary.com/dictionary/politics. Accessed November 10, 2016.

Selingo, Jeffrey J. "How the great recession changed higher education forever." *The Washington Post*, https//www.washingtonpost.com/education/2018/09/21/how-great-recession-changed-higher-education. Accessed September 21, 2018.

Seltzer, Rick. "New study attempts to show how much state funding cuts push tuition up." Inside Higher Education, https://insidehighered.com/print/news/2017/07/24/new-study-attempts-show-how-much-state-funding-cuts-push-up-tuition. Accessed 2017.

State Higher Education Officers. "SHEF: 2016 State Higher Education Finance". Boulder, CO. 2017

ABOUT THE AUTHOR

DR. ANDERES HAS spent much of his thirty-eight-year career in public higher education leadership positions, including the presidency in the Arizona Board of Regents; senior vice presidencies in Texas Tech University, the Oregon University System, the University of Wisconsin System, and the Connecticut Department of Higher Education; and being acting chancellor of the Nevada System of Higher Education. In those jobs, there was always a focus on financial decision-making, strategic planning, and connecting public policy to public higher education goals and outcomes. The areas of planning, financial decision-making, and public policy are the major themes in his papers and books.

He has written two additional books, *Navigating Through Turbulent Times: Applying a System and University Strategic Decision Making Model* (2015) and *Planning, Policy and Politics in Higher Education: Tools to Help Leaders Make Strategic Choices* (2016). Each book used the Strategic Decision-Making Model (SDMM) as the basis for looking at planning and decision-making in higher education from the perspective of leaders. The first book uses a real-life-example-based approach when conveying the application of the model. The second book focuses on a more in-depth analysis of each of the model components. This book goes one step further and emphasizes the defining roles and relationships of internal and external constituent politics in shaping the most significant decisions generated from competition and compromise.

Dr. Anderes taught undergraduate and graduate planning and financial courses at three universities and had numerous articles published in relevant higher education journals. He earned a PhD from the University of Connecticut and MPA and BA in political science from the University of Arizona.